HIRAM WILLIAMS

Exploring the Sources of His Expression

HIRAM WILLIAMS

EXPLORING THE SOURCES

OF HIS EXPRESSION

William B. Stephens

Memphis State University Press

For Avonell, Curt and Kim,

who know the subject best.

ISBN O-87870-045-5

Preface

In his "Random Jottings About Art" Hiram Williams said: "It would be comfortable to sit back knowing one could merely demonstrate a bit of technique and call oneself a painter; it would be comforting to know one were in command, but it does not work that way. Rather, we are at the beck and call of a dimly perceived idea which seduces us, beckoning us across swamps and pits and tangled briars, always fleeting ahead. And then we catch up to find it has been by our side all the time. We pause to catch our breath and it is gone." This comment is especially meaningful when used as a way of viewing an artist's moments of illumination. It is in that precise time of deciding what kind of line to put here or what kind of color to put there, that a moment of art happens. The artist is doing what no machine can do for him. His insights are a celebration of the creative mind at work.

This study of Hiram Draper Williams, painter and teacher of a generation of painters, lets the man himself speak as he probes into the realm of his self-awareness in the act of painting, and as he makes observations about himself and the effect of his past on his painting and teaching. At the same time, the study provides a psychologically critical examination of Williams' probe into the sources of his thought through dialogue, and an indication of some of the subconscious motivation of his painting while under hypnosis. It is an effort to appraise the personality and creative impulses of one of the most gifted and committed American painters living today.

The setting for the dialogue was the artist's home and studio in

Gainesville, Florida, a natural place for him to talk since it offered a setting where he trusted the situation, and had confidence in the relationships between himself, his materials, and the people around him. It was a place where cooperation could exist and he could talk freely about his own works which hung on the walls, and where he could examine the conflicts and symptoms of his impulses.

As it turned out, the procedures of assessment were linear in nature. The plan was for Williams to undergo extensive interviews preliminary to a painting experience under hypnosis. The key to the whole study was Williams' decision to cooperate. Many artists could not do this because their ego defenses would keep them from cooperating; they would not get into the situation; they would become detached from it to protect their self-feelings. Williams was asked to discuss his painting, to speak of his rationale for communicating inner and outer aspects of reality, and to express his intimate thoughts of people and their relationships.

Dr. Sol Kramer, a behavioral scientist on the faculty of the University of Florida Medical School, was enlisted in the project. His part was second only to that of the artist himself. Kramer was highly qualified for dealing with the problems of interviews; he was an authority on ethology, a trusted friend of Williams, and, over a period of five years, had "hung" one-man shows and helped in "Meet the Artist" interviews at the Sunken Meadow Life and Arts Center, Long Island, New York. In addition, Kramer had himself been under hypnosis and was familiar with hypnotic technique. As with Williams, Kramer worked at this project on a volunteer basis and in addition to his regular commitments.

The first interview was tape-recorded in the Williams' living room on 15 July 1971 and lasted about an hour and a half. The second interview continued along the vein of the first and was tape-recorded on 3 August 1971 in Williams' dining room and lasted almost two hours. The setting for the third interview was Stephens' apartment, where the talk concentrated on a collection of Williams' paintings and the difficulty of searching for an earlier motivation in painting. The third session was tape-recorded on 12 June 1972 and lasted about an hour. Although a copious flow of material had emerged through the interviews, all participants felt that the study should proceed to the planned hypnotic painting session.

A cameraman, Robert Beach, head of the Department of Medical Illustration at the University of Florida Medical School, was enlisted to film Williams' painting under hypnosis. So the fourth session was held in Williams' studio on 22 June 1972. The artist painted while in a mild hypnotic state. Because he was not asked to talk, only to paint, there are no remarks by the artist during his hypnotic state. The video tape made by Beach indicates the progression of the painting. Still photos in the book were taken from the television monitor. The only sounds recorded at the time were the swishing of brushes across an eight-foot canvas, the scraping of feet over the floor, and the cracking of ball bearings in spray cans as the paint was shaken. Remarks made by Williams immediately after the experiment are included.

A fifth session was autobiographical and was tape-recorded on Williams' patio on the morning of 8 April 1975. The artist was given a slip of paper with a few word cues on it and asked to talk about his early years. He talked for more than an hour without being interrupted or questioned. He had said many times in prior conversations that he put a value on the imaginative play, the stories and events of his boyhood, because they were formative and gave him a philosophy of life. It was these early years, he said, that helped him later to lead a fairly imaginative life.

The introduction includes a selection of the author's remembered experiences with the painter, and, I hope, offers further insights into the complexities of the artist's personality.

My appreciation is extended to others who in different ways contributed to the completion of this book. Special appreciation is entended to my brother, Dr. Robert O. Stephens of the University of North Carolina at Greensboro, for his constructive criticism and editorial help in piecing together the manuscript. Grateful appreciation is expressed to my wife, Jeanine, who typed the manuscript and who always encouraged and sacrificed when necessary, and who, along with my son, helped keep work in proper perspective by their humor and seriousness.

All information in the book, for which I am fully responsible, is the result of my research. It was a labor of love.

William B. Stephens
Texas Eastern University
Tyler, Texas   1978

Contents

Introduction

I became interested in Hiram Williams in 1954 soon after he joined the art faculty of the University of Texas at Austin. When I first knew him, he had very little money and drove an ancient blue Studebaker with a carrying rack on top, which had been purchased to move his furniture from California to Austin. The rack became useful thereafter to haul paintings around town. He was married and had children, worked day-long at the university, and painted with religious regularity at home every night. His paintings were large. One look at his paintings told me that he was an "Artist," an original. He spent lunch time painting while munching a sandwich. Classes over, he would paint again. At night he painted until he fell asleep over the easel.

He became conspicuous on the Texas campus although he was hidden from the painting majors because of his art methods classes. He vocalized the wonder that is the art of painting at every turn, and students from other classes were continually seeking his council; despite the demands of his teaching, he painted with the commitment and energy of a Van Gogh as he taught with the enthusiasm of a cheerleader. He was always on the move. A student said that he was "like a piece of popcorn on a hot griddle." His enthusiasm for art was immoderate. Consequently there was little demarcation between his living and his teaching. He once said his experience of the world and of art outside the classroom was the looking glass through which he viewed the problems of students. To some of Williams' colleagues, his behavior was more eccentric than his art. For a time he wore paint-splotched trousers, canvas-top shoes and sweat-soaked tee shirts to school. "Comfortable," he said. He was asked to make his appearance more presentable, whereupon he showed up early at school the next day wearing the most extreme of formal attire and planted himself just outside the departmental office door where everyone could see him. Williams was capable of being obnoxious.

To his Texan students, each Friday was "culture day." This meant student recitations, group singing, his spicy words of wisdom, and tomfoolery in general as Williams and students went about performing their assignments. These times were spontaneous and fruitful. Williams would sing, "Well, well, well, the well done gone dry." He said, "At the university, nervousness is frequently mistaken for zest." He once asked the class to imagine "what it is like to be a grasshopper on a hot afternnon." At times Williams would parody well known verse. An "Alice In Wonderland" kind of nonsense brightened up those Friday afternoons. He cultivated a sense of the bizarre to expand the thinking of the students as well as his own. He took his teaching and his art seriously despite the tom-foolery. He hoped to step beyond convention so that making odd connections might become habit.

He led conversations, never followed. He had a low threshold of boredom. As he talked, he frequently reconstructed his ideas. He spoke in rapid spurts, in a voice which he considered "tinny." His talk, as his art, tended toward fresh ideas. The momentum of what he had to say seemed to motivate further innovation. He expressed himself through streams of association.

Although Williams was nearing 40 years of age while in Texas, he looked much younger. To his considerable consternation he was frequently called "a promising young painter." Short in height, blue eyed, with crew cut hair, Williams' appearance belied the artist he was.

He painted in his carport, driveway, or living room. When friends visited to watch him paint, he would entertain them with recorded Alpine yodels or play "Lili Marlene," which reminded him of his war years. Visitors seemed not to bother him as he painted. He was angered by any reference to his likeness to Lautrec, for of necessity he stood on a chair to get at the top of one of his huge canvases.

Williams' first encounters with modern art occurred just after World War II while he was trying to work his way back into civilian life as a commericial artist in Philadelphia. He visited the Philadelphia Museum of Fine Arts many times to look at the works of Eakins and those he had a feeling for, but he ignored the works of Cézanne, Picasso, and other modern artists. An art instructor had prejudiced Williams against the modern movements. At long last he faced the fact that "modern art was here to stay," and decided to shirk his job one afternoon to go look at the Galletin Collection. "That was the best thing I ever did," he later said. There he discovered Alfred Barr's *Cubism and Abstract Art,* bought it, read it, and practically memorized it. He then began to paint cubist pictures to find out what made them work, which was another good thing he did for himself. He did not exhibit these paintings—he destroyed them—but the exercise provided an avenue for learning which helped him understand planes, shapes, fractures, and all the elements of modern formality.

Williams' preeminence in the art world was the result of his finding an image that held its own in competition and embodied his philosophy, an approach which continues to challenge him. He worked in the belief that a good talent could not go unnoticed over time. Still his ambition was identical to that of all careerists of the fifties: he wanted to make the art scene and make it big. The way to do that, he thought, was to have a body of work significantly different in order to establish a place for himself in the grand tradition of modern painting. He showed in the region: San Antonio, Dallas, Beaumont, and New Orleans. His work began to draw national attention. New talent scouts, movie celebrities, and art patrons began "to beat a path to his door." A movie actress visited his studio and said that she adored his art but wanted him to paint her a pretty picture. "I damn near spewed!" His reputation as an artist spread with each showing of his work.

The body of work that established Williams on the New York scene was begun under a faculty research grant, Project L-810, the first grant given by the University of Texas for creative work in painting. The initial painting in the series was an overhead view of a marching figure, stretched as though it were elastic. The prototype for the overhead figure had been painted in 1950, of a stretched male nude, which had been destroyed but not forgotten. Williams worked with both seated and standing figures always depicted in elevation. The Texas grant brought time for Williams to search for the best within himself, but what he found was not really recognized until he moved to Florida.

Shortly after I met Williams at the University of Texas, he invited me to his house to discuss questions I had about my own work. One thing led to another, and soon at his invitation I began bringing my canvases and we worked as we talked.

A friendship grew. I came to know his family. His wife Avonell worked as a secretary in the university graduate school and tutored her children, Curtis Earl and Kim, after supper and on weekends. They confided to me their day's adventures as they dangled from my knee. Curt had a room stocked with hamsters and white mice. He also had an affinity for wet earthworms. Kim's room contained a large doll house mounted on a desk. Kim loved felines, large and small, and the entire family doted on a dog which brought catches of chewed rabbit to the back door.

The Williamses took a trip north to visit parents and in-laws in Pennsylvania each summer without fail. They made the trips through sunshine and downpour, in outmoded cars sporting faulty radiators, worn gaskets, worn tires, and cracked blocks. Once they had a wreck in New Bern, North Carolina. These trips were made during their vacation period. Williams resented these excursions, for they cut into painting time. Williams had also made one trip alone—the flight to his father's funeral. He gave this account of the trauma:

> . . . you are at 26,000 feet, lightning flares reveal cumuli towering another 20,000 above. You are there because your brother phoned you at 2:00 a.m. In forty-eight hours the funeral director will tell you that "he's holding up good. Thought he might stink by now." Discovery: It's as hard to lose one's father at 40 as it is at 14!

In the summer of 1962 Williams packed his family to Estella,

Pennsylvania, and camped in a field on a farm which had once belonged to his father-in-law. Although the trips could be construed as family duty, the following letter indicated that there were rewards:

July 22, 1962

Dear Bill:

It is night. I am seated before a chair which holds this typewriter. The night is wet. Great sheets of water poured over us all day long. We live in two tents and I paint in another erected upon a platform I built at cost of bunged up fingers and other injuries too numerous to mention. But now the painting goes well. I've gotten a grip upon another and new version of the figure. It looks good to me, and I hope I'm right. At this juncture in my career I'd better not fumble.

Syracuse University wanted me, but I turned them down. The move would not have paid me well enough, so you see I am a materialist after all. I'll go back to Florida and think of the big cold snows in the North next winter.

The skunks and coon raid our food supply. The deer roil our spring. The field mice fall into it and drown. A bear and her cubs are wandering somewhere nearby. It is all great and I'm delighted to be alive. We are well and how are you all?

Regards from Hiram and family

Williams' fame increased rapidly through the 1960s. The Museum of Modern Art bought *The Challenging Man,* the Whitney Museum of American Art acquired *Gazing Man,* and *Incubus* became part of the National Collection of Fine Arts at the Smithsonian Institution, Washington, D.C. Regional museums and universities across the country also added Williams' paintings to their collections, while newspapers, magazines, and journals further extended his reputation and recognition. In 1965 his letters, diaries, and other papers were requested for the Archives of American Art. In those years between 1960 and 1969 I saw Williams only a few times. We lived far apart and our correspondence was spotty, but I followed his career with keen interest as I read about him in magazines and inquired of him from those who had seen him. He kept me posted with notes and the biannual invitations to his New York shows. Finally, I determined to earn an advanced degree in professional education at Gainesville.

Summer 1969: "Welcome to the University of Williams at Gainesville, Florida," wrote a mutual friend of ours. Not long after I got my family settled in an apartment, Williams handed me a key to his studio. Inside he pointed to shelves of paint and gave me a large, newly-stretched canvas. He marked a line across the floor and warned: "On this side is my territory, on that side is yours. I'm posting submachine guns at each end, so don't dare step across."

Williams' personality had not changed in the nine years that he had been in Florida, but he was noticeably aging. His hair was longer, his waistline more expansive. He was a middle-aged painter of 52. He described himself at his worst in an essay, "Myself As A New Ruin": "smelly of breath and armpit, runny nose, cracked of voice; a series of connected pains in the chest, solar plexus, groin, thighs, knees, feet and liver." He also complained of "nauseous back pains precisely where my lungs meet my kidneys. I have sensations of clogged cells in my brain, caused by dense white and pink vapors which originate somewhere within two feet of my buttocks and then somehow work up my spinal column. I have scaley skin sloughing shreds of weathered paste and I have dandruff so aged that it has turned yellow. Blow flys follow me about eager to lay maggot eggs. My teeth are bad. This is even true of several of them that happen to be false." Williams's problems were compounded by fasting during the day and resorting to heavy dinners with cocktails at night. From time to time his wife directed him to diets.

He had built a large white, black-trimmed, stucco house which stood under an acre of loblolly pines. There were no windows on the front or street side of the residence (to the confusion of some who fancied it a gangster hide-out). A set of black, wooden, double doors centered the front. These doors opened upon an enormous room which served both as living room and gallery. The floor of Alabama white marble was in near collapse from the weight of Williams' pride in it. The studio was in the northeast quadrant of the house. Another source of pride was that he had bought the land with sales of his paintings. His first New York "one-man" had been a sell-out.

Two welded sculptures spotted the yard, student work. On the west side of the house stretched the apron of a concrete patio. Over that he hoped to cultivate an arbor which would extend over a swimming pool. He took unalloyed joy in his place and walked its perimeter, calling it his "estate." The route to the Williams house was down a quarter mile of sandy road the width of a car.

Williams did what he could to make life interesting. At one party he ate an egg, shell and all. At another party he suggested that everyone there become blood brothers, Indian style! There was no contest, and he was to spend an uncomfortable week as his finger healed. One Saturday morning people were eyeing the lot next door. Williams ruffled his clothes and hair, clutched a whiskey bottle in one hand, and went out to meet them. The sale fell through.

Williams took his success in stride. His achievements contradicted the myth that an artist must live a Bohemian life-style in New York City, London, or the West Coast to "make it" in the art world. It was "specious to presume that an artist had to live in a hovel or a rat's heap in order to make art," he said. In a letter he once said that a professor envying his success told him that he was merely shrewd. "The poor fellow couldn't imagine honest dealings and honest results in the art world. Success must be built on clever operation, he thought" (5/23/62). Williams' personal definition of success required that he paint a body of work constituting a coherent vision, the "world of Hiram Williams."

He resisted being identified with a movement. He recognized the influence of other artists on his early career and regretted it. He meant to match the work of the best artists while using his own terms, and to compete with them in the quality of their accomplishment: "Artists know those who have established a pace and one identifies with the standard and precedent which they have achieved. This knowledge helps give worth to what one is doing, even as one is denying them." Once at the Gainesville airport, while waiting for Williams to board a plane, I asked how he answered those who inquired of his style: "I just tell them I am a modern artist; I paint modern pictures in a modern manner" (4/29/70). He worked within boundaries of form which govern the Williams' look. Today he might be influenced by other artists' concepts but never by their imagery.

When asked about his self-image as a celebrated painter, Williams said, "I think of myself as a person with inhibitions, with a respository of concepts that are not my own, and yet to be an artist I must find concepts of form unique and personal. The artistic type is passive emotionally. I really have no desire to be a leader or have leadership of projects. I prefer bizarre projects where I am not under imposed control; where there is no standard by which to be measured. I'm pragmatic and tend to do the expedient, to act in the terms of crisis rather than in the terms of planning. I play much by ear—a lot of things that don't have to be played at all, I might add. It is a chore for me to do what can be done by routine" (7/3/71).

Williams had made the table and benches where we often sat and talked. He had sawed the planks, hammered the nails, and painted them. When it came to carpentry, Williams said his approach was to achieve expression while subordinating the craft. "I take the direct and easiest means to get to it. I have an impatience with doing the time-consuming," he said while building the couch to place before his "Corcoran" piece in the living room. Williams made cabinets to hold objects and built places to sit. He keyed in on the environment—a ceiling beam or a room corner—to shape his furniture. He said, "If it were not for my paintings I would be quite indifferent to the house; I feel that these rooms are only adjuncts to my painting." The wooden furniture was black in stark contrast to the white walls, a Shaker influence. Friends were invited to carve their names on a kitchen cabinet. The premises seemed alive with people: students, relatives, dignitaries. Visiting the Williams family homestead became a continuing adventure for me.

What does Williams say that has not been said already? "You know when we examine literature it is not the comedies that stand out as significant works, it is the tragedies: these get at the truth. And I hope my art is getting at the truth. Maybe it does. The statements of my paintings are hard for most people to take. Truth is always hard to take."

When it came time for me to leave Gainesville and take on a new job, the Williamses invited my family to drop by for breakfast on our way out of town. It was a sad occasion for several reasons, not the least of which was the fact that their dog, Skip, had become riddled with cancer. So Williams borrowed a rifle and shot it. We dug a grave behind the pony barn, wrapped the dog in one of Williams' old canvases, and buried it. Truth is hard.

Three Interviews

The following three chapters are interviews between Williams and Sol Kramer, an ethologist and member of the behavioral science division of the University of Florida Department of Psychiatry, who was also interested in the instinctive and motivational elements of Hiram Williams' style.

Interview

Williams' Living Room
15 July 1971

Kramer: Maybe we ought to start with something very simple, like a definition and the function of art as you see it. Do you think that is an appropriate question?

Williams: Yes, and the answer I have formulated is as much for myself as for my students. The role of the artist is to devise a world of form, utilizing a vocabulary that is of his formulation—one having associational relations with the phenomenal world. It is the artist's job, as I see it, to stake out an area of expression and then pursue this endeavor to the end of his career. What he contributes is a world of form that should be uniquely his. My personal desire is to create a world that is a metaphor of the phenomenal world, and I insist that it be communicable to any intelligent viewer that happens to encounter it. As a result of their encounter with the world that I offer through form, I hope viewers will somehow gain a larger understanding, and therefore, an extended grasp of the world they inhabit. I agree with Irwin Edman in his belief that "art is to vitalize life, underlying the emotional aspects of life." I learned what I have just said during a visit to a show held at the Los Angeles County Museum in those days located on Exposition Boulevard. There I saw three galleries of Miró—early, middle, to late Miró—and as I looked at the consistency of his work, its progression and change of form as he worked over years, I could literally feel my own life extended. The feel of it was palpable. I could feel it then, and I am benefited to this day. I tell students, "If you had never known the world of Paul Klee, of course, you would not know what you had missed; but now that you know the world of Paul Klee, think how much he has added to the dimension of your personal world." And this, it seems to me, is the task of the artist—to create a vision that adds dimension to the emotional life and memory of his fellowman.

Kramer: Hiram, let me go back to two things you said. You indicated that the artist has to pursue something, and commit himself to something that is unique to him. And then a little later you said something about the fact that you want to communicate to other people. How do you juxtapose these two conceptions of something unique, and at the same time something communicative to other people? Is there something about that uniqueness which, nevertheless, is meaningful and contains basic themes which are communicative in spite of the uniqueness.

Williams: I can speak to that. I would suspect that the sculptor, Brancusi, somehow began to understand (perhaps because of the prior examples of painters, Malevich, Kandinsky, and others) that form itself had implications. He pursued this in the "Madam Pogony" series. For example, abstract shapes, which, you remember, were almost egg-like, were derived from a model's features. He went on eventually to more and more abstract sculptures, less descriptive of objects in the real world—the reality of form substituting for descriptive reality.

Anyway, Brancusi aside, I do agree that artistic creation in what many of us call the nonobjective area is both viable and rewarding. I've had phases of working abstractly, but by and large, my work has been descriptive—representative. This is probably the result of conditioning—perhaps originating when a teenager named John Morse taught me (I was in sick bed at five or six years of age) to draw a wolf's and a horse's head. My parents marveled at my ability to emulate John Morse's example. Later, at age eight, I was placed in Mrs. Luce's art class. She was 83 years old—a painter of flowers in

Titusville, Pennsylvania—and she taught children via formal art lessons. She was, of course, an entirely descrptive painter; it was heavy conditioning for youngsters.

The adolescent stage of growth is a highly descriptive period. I do not believe that any adolescent would make an abstraction of his own free will. He's too concerned to show his interest in rockets and airplanes. She is too concerned about dresses. I can argue that a continued interest in descriptive art and the doing of it is simply retardation, a continuing adolescent viewpoint. That well may be one of my problems. I've been told by many, including my wife, to grow up!

My peculiar concern for form stems from what must have been a homosexual phase, an interest during late adolescence in the human body—in particular, my own. Narcissism. I lived for Michelangelo and Rubens and their art. In that period I was much engaged with gymnastics, and I wasn't a bad tumbler, if I do say so myself. I was small, but I was a pretty muscular fellow. I wasn't big enough to really compete in football and other games, but I was mighty interested in physical prowess. I also recall being interested in girls. I crept away and made secret drawings of sex parts and love making.

Kramer: How old were you then?

Williams: Oh, I suppose 14, 15, 16. I lived in a house that was asexual, because Dad was a Baptist preacher, and someone like Mother didn't count. It was a house without women, and I had these impulses. I took care of them as best I could. This, of course, Sol, brings me to something that I think would make an interesting study. I have often wondered how much of the fine draftsmanship, particularly in the figurative areas, was developed as boys made secret pornographic drawings? I have thought that this may be a difference between men and women. As you know, few women artists seem notably involved with figurative art. Is it because women are not visually oriented sexually, and therefore haven't practiced the pornographic drawing that later shores up the male artist's figurative work? I surmise that some of the best art on earth is probably in the Vatican; some of it at Indiana University, but I would guess the larger share of such art has been destroyed or hidden, not made available, out of shame. Because, if art is expression, some of the most expressive art would necessarily emerge from the intense drive we experience as sexuality.

Kramer: Then you link this secretive period with an expression of the fineness of detail and strong emotionality. Are you suggesting that these two things have a relationship?

Williams: I haven't discussed this subject with my fellow artists, male or female. However, I've seen enough of myself in relationship to other males to expect my experience to have been theirs. Our behavior patterns and our desires are not significantly different. So, if I followed this pattern, it is impossible for me to believe that others haven't followed the same pattern—Michelangelo, or whoever.

Kramer: Hiram, I'd like to pursue this question of uniqueness and communication. I think it is quite central to the art process, and art as a function. You have found a way of viewing the reality of people and the world about you. What you pursue is unique to you, but nevertheless it has some particular, broad, communicative value about basic relationships for other people. I think this is what provides dialogue between the artist and the viewer. One of the things that is said today is that art is an institution; but of course, art as an institution grew out of somebody secretively (maybe just like you said) beginning to make little representations. And it was this tendency to make little representations, long before we had written language, that others in the social community found meaningful. Man's innate capacity for symbolic thought and communication is reflected every night in his dreams. This grew into the institution that we call art today, which has become such a vital part of the human social system. But, it grows out of the individual. Art is something that comes out of the individual, and, like all forms of expression, has some general aspects that are communicative and meaningful to other individuals.

With that as background, I would like to ask why you chose the particular subjects you have been painting for as long as I have known you. For example, the chap with many arms, with many mouths, with many smiles (false or otherwise). Now, you may have started with other themes, but how did you happen to choose that particular subject, and why was it meaningful to you?

Williams: What I've been expressing is my predilection for the human figure and the human being. Along with this is a recognition that my concern is not for form alone—it never has been. My concern is for *us*. I suspect that this is an outgrowth of exposure to the Western art tradition where the human figure from the time of Renaissance has been emblemized as being the most important image with which an art person could deal. So, in the WPA days, when I was exposed to art teaching, the human figure was the paramount form. This was the one image one got serious about in the thirties. I feel this way to this day. I think it is based upon what I said earlier about relationships of form through myself. There was, as you know, a period following World War II when Abstract Expression was the art form in America—and I was an Abstract Expressionist. I found that I was adroit and readily picked up the "action" approach to painting. I found that it was remarkably easy. And, to me, it soon became remarkably meaningless. That meant, then, that I had to do the obvious—that I was forced to return to tradition, to the figure. I had the wit to look for problems having to do with the figure, for this is something that the 20th century has taught us—that an artist approaches his art through problems. One doesn't say to himself, "I wish to communicate to this person or that person or to any hundreds of people." The artist must engage a problem. Inevitably the problem is related to "the period vision" of the day. Because it is always so that either you are reacting against the period (which means you have turned your back utterly upon the semblances of the time) or, what is more likely, you try to engage the times by having a problem that is in some way reflective of the times. In my case, I pondered what Cézanne and the Cubists had accomplished with the figure, and I eventually came to this idea: I would show the totality of the human figure without fracturing it, as had Cézanne and the Cubists. This would make my art different. In the 20th century anything that has difference expressively has had consequent validity. We have all felt this. I think today it is a specious notion of which entirely too much has been made, but I am telling you about my experience and this is the way it was. The human figure not being just me, but *us*, became something I was aware of early. I launched into what I call the "overhead" figures and the "guilty" figures, etc. Every image I've painted was painted as a result of an actual encounter, out of my sense of *me*. For example, when I painted the "guilty"—while pinning down the good and evil in man—I knew perfectly well I was imaging myself. When I paint a scurrying man, a man running, this is me—the tension lies in me, sometimes to the level of trauma. I express what is in all of us. Just as I assume that if I did dirty little pictures as a young artist, other artists have done so, I assume without question that if I feel good and evil, my interior torn, others do also. And the reason that I make a point of this is that, since it is a common experience, it can be read by viewers. I report on all of us. The reportage as an artist—you know, I was once called an "angst" figurative painter, a painter of anxieties, human anxieties—I am a reporter of calamity. For example, if I paint a bloody faced "Doomed Man" I am openly voicing my own fear of death, unquestionably relieving myself in a catharsis. Probably much of what I do, like much of art, is filling in that interval between now and my demise, my death. I think a lot of human activity stems from this compulsion—and I think it should in my particular case. I think this is certainly the case with Bacon, with a lot of deKooning's work, with a lot of art. I am saying that as I do paint these images I have an awareness of communication with every man-jack that thinks about these things at all.

Kramer: Then, the reality of your painting grows out of the reality of something within yourself, and your being in touch with that aspect of reality. In a sense, although your subject matter is unique, it is at the same time also "realistic" in that it reflects an on-going process in you.

Williams: Yes, that's right. Sol, you have used the words real and reality, which I believe and preach in my teaching, that we drive for truth, we in art. We strive for a reality. Through technique, through imagery, a surrogate for the real world, or even imagery that is only form for form's sake, we strive for something we can think of as ultimate truth. Truth that is not measurable. This is a truth that corresponds to our emotional sense for what is so.

Kramer: Truth not generally acceptable, or truth not generally known?

Williams: I don't think there is any news in my truth. For example, I have here a painting I call "Sexual Tension." Probably a stupid title, but at least it is a very direct one. It is about a couple living with their sexual needs. This is a pressure upon any so-called normal human being. It is constant, up to late and even older age.

Kramer: We are getting more expression of the sex life of the 60- year old, the 70- and 80-year-olds.

Williams: Yes. At 54 I'm delighted! But, now, I think you would agree with me that the way I cast the idea has a startling aspect—even though I don't think I'm saying anything in this painting that is news. I don't think I'm making a mark, an image, or apparition that you don't recognize out of hand. In short, all I think I'm doing is underlining your experience, my experience, man's experience. And, I think that any goodness, and the calibration of my work outside the formal quality, should be valued on how well I do this. Francis Bacon paints figures, and he has made comments that he is painting not *of* experience but *creates* experience. He says he wants to have in a canvas the feeling of something human having crawled across it, leaving a slime, like a snail. He has made that comparison. I have read essays pointing out that Bacon used wounded figures, crippled figures, and that kind of thing. But you know none of these touch what he is really doing, because what he is really doing is painting trauma. He is painting that moment of truth, that moment when the hypodermic needle is mainlined. Ultimate moments for the flesh. I think he is successful, because he is so successful at doing just this. For example, while Edward Hopper speaks that, "All I've ever tried to do is paint the way light strikes a wall," I think Hopper hasn't begun to tell us what he has really done. What he is *always* doing is telling us about wasted lives. Here is a sexually potent, nubile woman in a room alone. There is not going to be a visitor. He paints a balcony scene near the seacoast in Maine, and there stands an older man and woman, parents of an extremely voluptuous girl in a swim suit. You know, again, that nothing is going to come of this. Wasted flesh. Remember "Night Work At The Office." Here is a man dressed in his buttoned-down collar, huddled over a desk. A most voluptuous woman stands by the filing cabinet. It is obviously well into the night. And yet, one understands that nothing is going to come of this—a betrayal of one another by reason of the fact of not filling out their real needs. Now, it is in this sense that we could go on to the obvious, to Morris Graves' "Bird Singing in the Moonlight," a surrogate for the human spirit, etc., etc. Painters are very frequently not painting the object. What one must search for is the subject. Do I make myself clear?

Kramer: I think that you are getting into an area (when you talked about Bacon and putting something on canvas) that reflects what is human—your emphasis on these areas of emotionality and sexuality. Are you saying that there are many areas, many aspects of what human beings do, what they feel, that are being overlooked, dehumanized by the times and the way we live today? And that part of the function, as far as communication on the part of the artist is concerned, is to keep other human beings aware through this unique contact with his own feelings and his ability to explore this reality and convey it to other individuals; to keep this aspect of being human on the surface, in spite of all the other kinds of technological, industrial and machine-like and computerized aspects of society that are developing. That at this point in time, our communicative processes (including non-communication) are what motivate you? Hiram, is what I have said relevant as far as your work is concerned?

Williams: Certainly. Perhaps we'd better indicate that I represent a certain breed of artist. I think of myself as a humanist and my concern is with us and society. I would never be a propagandist. I feel that you can never have propaganda and have art at the same time. I think many good talents have gone up in smoke because of this misunderstanding. It was a grave fault in the Mexican muralists, Orozco and company.

Kramer: You don't deliberately set out to counteract what is going on in society; but what you do is simply maintain contact with something that is going on within yourself, something that is a problem or an area of concern to you.

Williams: I am aware that I am reiterating the stuff that has been said in Occidental art from the beginning. I know full well I'm not saying

interpreted as being the emotional experience—isn't that the real experience the artist endeavors? He doesn't depict a photographic representation, but a representation which is mixed with his own real emotional reaction to it.

Williams: Yes! That's right Sol, but there he insisted upon the representation because *there* was the reality.

Kramer: That was one branch of reality and the other branch was his reaction to that reality and the blending of the two. Now, when you talk about collage, people think of bits of newspapers. I know one chap (Sam Middleton, now a well-known "Dutch" artist) who took Mexican newspapers, tickets from theater, bull-fights, tram cars, etc., and colored them into his own black experience because they, too, represented his real experiences. We are talking about reality again. I had never thought about this strong endeavor of the artist to stay with reality—some aspect of reality, however mundane.

Williams: What I'm trying to say here, Sol, is that with these efforts to see, reality began to be, for me, a stable object copied—no longer real. It was real in the sense that I had been conditioned as a young artist under Mrs. Luce, but in an intellectual sense I understood that we don't understand the world this way. I'm not so sure that my relationship with the world was so dramatically different from Grandad's. After all, I haven't become multi-emotioned and multi-faceted myself. Even today, as I ride in an airplane going through time and space, I'm not sure this is such a tangibility for an organism such as myself.

When John Glenn completed his first orbit and landed, he went to church the following Sunday—and, from what I hear and read of him, I'm not so sure he has become more emotionally tuned to time and space. (He hurt his back slipping in a bathtub. At that moment Glenn found where it was at!)

But conceptually, we all begin to understand, as we view the 20th century, that the truth of our time lies in a time-space relationship. So in art one tries to pin down what one intellectually views as truth. For example, you speak of my multi-armed men. Never for a moment, not for a second, do I think of them as being multi-armed, as in art representing a Hindu god. To me, even though I connect multiple arms, these to me represent continuous movements through space; and, as far as the image goes, what I offer is movement without Cubist fracturing.

Cubists, the Futurists, all fractured. If this aspect of my contribution amounts to anything, it amounts enough to give my work an essential difference; whatever importance that has I don't know. Still the fact that I don't fracture does make for a difference. The intellectual thought was that we move through space.

Kramer: Hiram, let me ask how that applies to the painting "Doomed Man" in which you have two mouths. Does that represent two positions of an aspect of surprise or horror at the bloodiness of death or whatever? Two successive positions?

Williams: Intellectually I understand the 20th century predilection for movement through space and time—I accept this; I come to a problem; and I resolve it. Now I would have not gone with it a bit further, nor would any artist go a bit further, if there was anything to him at all, if emotional needs were not met. I had a hunch that the stroboscopic man was saying more about 20th-century man than if I had painted a single walking figure, rather than a strobe image.

Kramer: What do you feel that figure is saying that is more than just a single-mouthed individual? In some of your figures you have a single eye. We know that also is a contradiction because there are two eyes. By putting in one, you are asking us to look at a human being in another light. You're supplying another facet to our understanding of what a person is like—you most certainly succeed with this painting of yours.

But I would like to know, in words, what those two mouths mean as far as you're concerned; what additional affective motif it provides for you.

Williams: Now I think we come to a truth of art! Bacon, the Elizabethan, once writing about playwriting, said there had to be a twist in a play.* He meant that you present an event through the

---

*"There is no excellent beauty without some strangeness in the proportion." Francis Bacon (1561-1626), "Of Beauty."

form of the play and somewhere there had to be something singular happen, some unexpected happening to give expression to the play.

William Merrit Chase, a very prominent teacher of art in this country, circa World War I, used the word "queering." He would teach his students to "queer." He would insist that they paint objects while transforming the image to heighten the expression of the object. I think this holds water—Picasso's "the lie that makes the truth," you know. When we observe these two mouths and a certain distortion of the head, we simply gain metaphorically. It becomes somehow more real, at least it is so to me.

Kramer: You are saying that your two mouths function almost as an eye catcher, or something that makes the viewer stay with the figure. You also depict bloodiness, etc., etc. You are conveying several things. You are conveying, on the one hand, death, the destruction, the bloodiness of an individual. We see death around us all the time, but if you portrayed death as Munch did, or one's sudden immediate demise, people might turn away. But what you are saying, then, is that the two mouths almost compel one to stay with that feeling. You can't turn away, and the reason you can't turn away is not because of the aspect of death, but because of the two mouths—and then you have to consider and look at it. Are you saying, thereby, that you have to have something to catch and hold people to art? That people are too quick to turn away from this scene?

Williams: I'd say this is true of all art that has maintained—the reality of it is something of the nature we are discussing. The intense focus in the chiaroscuro of Rembrandt is most necessary. Remove chiaroscuro from Rembrandt and what you would have, I don't know. A method to achieve pictorial intensity—makes unusualness—this is not in the real world. Of course, back to something you said earlier, to me this is one mouth in two different places, that's all, just as those several arms on my "Theologian." If I felt that I were making a 50-armed theologian, I couldn't do it! The viewer must simply accept that this is a theologian in different places.

Kramer: How do you relate this to something else we talked about earlier, Hiram—your canvases which are eight-and-one-half feet tall and your figure which (if it stood up) would be about 14 feet tall? That very size alone forces one to stay with the canvas; I think you do stay with a 14-foot figure in front of you, more than with an 18-inch figure on a three-foot canvas.

Williams: That's right, and this fact, the readiness with which I do this might not be surprising if we stop to think of the kind of visual sensations current in our time—the Three-D movie, the out-size screen, the giant screen. My God, we see a couple kissing and all we see are their chins—their mouth about their noses—and they are 15 feet high. We accept this. Real blockheads, who would jeer modern art, will sit in a movie and watch this really grotesque event and never murmur—and it is as real to the guy as the girl sitting beside him. The idea of making large paintings is nothing new in art. Down in Sarasota there are enormous Rubens. But, of course, I know that they were originally meant to stand rather high on the wall. The Sistine Chapel figures are enormous because of the height of the building, and so forth. I have a suspicion that we can do this sort of thing (paint out-sized figures that are viewed fairly close up—within a viewing distance of 15 feet) and have them much more acceptable as reality today. You know I told you earlier that I've yet to have anybody come along and complain about the size of my paintings or suggest that they are not very real. I think it is so because they are conditioned. Our sense of scale, in the sense that Grandad might have had, is obliterated by outdoor movies, Three-D screens, billboards—this constant manifestation of out-size scale. We have changed our sense of scale. And, I think I am taking advantage of the fact that we don't accept scale as we once did. We introduce a new order of reality in painting, via scale.

Kramer: Hiram, you painted stroboscopic man. After that, I believe, you began to depict women in many dimensions—first on an orthodox canvas and then you went from the area of the canvas to beyond the canvas, or to doing away with the canvas. Do you want to say something about that?

Williams: I have wondered about all this very much myself. The first thing (to put it in a fairly logical order) one can see by looking at the paintings is a progression of the form. We are looking at the way a form develops when one deals with form—the form of a female in this case.

Kramer: Let me ask you one quick question here. Do you know any special reason why you went from the depiction of the huge male form to the female form?

Williams: I can explain quickly. I can say to you that I am traditional, but that I agreed with myself when I left Abstract Expressionism to return to tradition to attempt to transform its subject matter.

I do landscapes; I do still lives; I do figures, male and female. So there is no mystery. As the form developed, I fancied I was coming upon the new, particularly when I came upon the "Chorus Lines." But there is no true newness. I remember that Steve Lotz came by one day after I was well into the "Chorus Lines," and he leafed a book he had found of Oriental art. He showed me, in a book by Jurs, some pictures of multi-breasted females in Indian art. Both images came as a complete surprise to me.

To examine how I came to paint "Chorus Lines": I had based my art upon a single figure in multiple views; now I turned the problem around. This is one of those things that happens in the artist's psyche and seems beyond explanation. The best I can say is that one day I awoke to another approach to the figure: the idea to treat a crowd as though it were one organism, one figure, was the "Chorus Line" which eventually led to the cut-out figures. Of course, this meant multi-breast and multi-bellies, and multi-crotches. Formally, lots of promise there. Nipples could act as points. Bellies could be treated to be extremely plastic. The bellies are marvellous because of the sensation of an indeterminate surface coming forward and going back—makes for a very alive feeling, formally alive, that is. I realized early that some women of my acquaintance didn't like my paintings. That didn't matter. Men came by. They didn't say much. My own regard was that "this is where I am. I've got to do my work this way. One must follow where one's ideas lead."

Kramer: What drives you to say, "This is where I am, I've got to do it?" What sense of subject?

Williams: Because of form! The idea had opened up to this. Ideas in art are much too precious to cast aside. One must push them through to the end. There must be a fierce cause before an artist drops an idea.

I once found in myself a desire to paint "Earth Mothers," which is understandable in my case. In mythic lore such creatures are very real. And I've been surrounded by women all through my later life—mother, two aunts, my wife, her three sisters, my mother-in-law. Oh, there has been my brother with whom I've had a distant relationship; a father who was almost a figure removed, up in his study; and then Curt (son); and male friends like yourself. But it is incredible how much of my later life has women in it, not as sexual playmates, but just women—in their menopause, most of them.

Kramer: You might say asexual women.

Williams: That's correct; so many of them are asexual. That is correct. Here is the classical hang-up: you will find no time when I will paint the female organs. I don't have a real feeling that I need to do so. The breast, the belly, yes. One would think I would have a terrible predilection for the crotch, as I do for the belly and the breast. I sometimes wonder what kind of veil is being drawn.

Now, when I come to painting the male, I have no desire to show male parts at all. None at all. Do I find my background is such that I can't? Do I feel it would be masturbation in public, that sort of thing? Perhaps at that point I come too close to me.

Kramer: Hiram, let's return to the theme you mentioned in regard to anatomical aspects of the human figure. The fact that you find yourself readily portraying breasts and bellies. But about the vaginal area—you said that you are not quite as drawn to that area and that you don't depict it in as much detail as breasts and belly areas.

It occurred to me that some artists have said that when they are doing a painting they feel themselves in the painting. So I'm wondering to what extent your involvement with the breast area or the belly area is something you have a very close feeling for. Along the same line, why do you stay away from the vaginal area of the woman and depict that as a general, sort of shadowy region, or a black region as you have done in your last two paintings here? You have taken the pubic area and you have made it black, whereas the breast and belly area is red and vivid.

Williams: I have a notion that the rationale that governs this is that in imaging breast and belly we have a universal symbol of fecundity, of nurture and nourishment, and so forth. It has identities other than just sexual. I know that I don't want to paint paintings that are simply pornographic. My concern is not there, and I am very clear with myself that this is so.

Kramer: I never think of your paintings as pornographic, but has anybody ever reacted to your paintings from that angle?

Williams: Never. If anything, it's been asexual. The women react and obviously identify sometimes, and they don't like what they are identifying with, with boobs, etc.

When it comes to the figure itself, I tell students drawing from life that when they have completed drawing a thigh, for instance, they should feel their thighs aching from tenseness. If they do not feel this, it proves they haven't really been with it. I much believe in this.

One of the reasons we have nudes in art is because we see clothing as a concealment of the real us. And I suppose that if we take our clothing off, the real us is not there—the real us is even deeper inside. Nevertheless, this is about the best we can do.

Kramer: It is an aspect of reality normally veiled.

Williams: That is correct, and so artists have never hesitated to take the clothes off their images. The drive toward reality—truth governs this. On the other hand, I've never had a wish to paint a pair engaged in intercourse, because, somehow, this would be too illustrational to me. You notice these paintings have presence; they project forward psychically out of the canvas and, I hope, into the orbit of your mind. Mine is an art of confrontation, by and large. The intent is to move out of the canvas into the room with the viewer. I wish for both a formal and psychically compelling image.

Kramer: Maybe that is a better way of putting what we tried to say before, namely of holding the viewer or spectator. You talk about moving out. Is this another way of making contact?

Williams: I am allied with Bacon, in that I am not interested at all to depict experience. *I want to cause the viewer to experience my art.*

Your confrontation with my art is a dual affair. It's confronting you as you confront it, and *that* is the experience. There is a kind of painting that doesn't confront us—one the viewer must move into optically. For example, when viewing Pollock's maze one moves into the interstices, in and out. This is what I call "an event."

Kramer: We are experiencing movement as we scan?

Williams: Just so. I want my painting to be the real world. I think I want it to be of the real world just as you are of the real world. In this sense I play God.

Kramer: You talk about interrogating yourself, start asking yourself questions; this is a constant isn't it, in your painting?

Williams: All the time.

Kramer: Something goes on, then you begin to react to what you put there, don't you?

Williams: I am the first viewer of my painting. Sometimes I erase things at the moment. And I've wondered at this, Sol—how many paintings of real worth have been eradicated by the artist because he, himself, couldn't stand it as the first viewer?

Kramer: That's an interesting thought, isn't it. Well, what I want to get to is, when you question yourself in that way, does that questioning lead to another mode, another style in a painting? I have a feeling that you have questioned yourself in this way, but that it doesn't alter the mode of expression at the time. It may matter two years later, or three years later. The reason I say this is because I find you completing a series all along the same vein and theme. You've got five canvases eight-and-one-half feet tall and you develop a theme, but all this time this questioning goes on. Is that what you are saying? What happens then? You work out the answer to the question in the process of painting, or do you work out the answer, or does the painting work out the answer? What happens in that process as you question yourself in paint?

Williams: The questions concern the problem, defining interior formal and descriptive problems that arise, all of them requiring answers in paint. I have questions about depiction of genitals when I paint the figure. How do I paint so that the viewers' eyes register elsewhere than at the crotch, and so on. Because the concern is that these are not sexual figures. The concern is with human beings—a man and a woman. Yes, I'm much more concerned with these as human beings than I am with them as sexual beings.

Kramer: Don't the two go together; they are part and parcel?

Williams: Yes. I can't deny that.

Kramer: It is so difficult for an individual or one artist, to tell another artist what he should or what he should not put into a work.

Williams: The matter of decision-making, too, is a nebulous procedure. I suspect that what I'm going to say could be carried into all sorts of areas, but I'll confine it to painting. I think I've said it to you—I think of painting as a dialogue; you're talking to the image, and it's talking to you. You decide to do something, and then the painting informs you to do such and such, or to make a change, and so it goes. And, then, I think I've told you of how the artist approaches it as a destructive, as well as the constructive man. That is why I think a painter can paint areas very carefully, then for no conceivable reason wipe out, or, suddenly maddened, kick the picture. Later the poor chap cannot reconstruct why he was mad in the least—very childish sort of behavior can occur. I think the destructive and the constructive man are of the same coin. That is why I think the painter can turn to violence so easily while working. And then, of course, we are both concerned with the fact that there is the rational and the irrational man, operational at the same time. All of this is involved with the "dialogue."

Kramer: Hiram, let me interrupt you and make a suggestion at this point. This business of making a decision in painting, of what you will put in and what you won't put in, I think is quite interesting in itself. I'd like to suggest that we go into the living room and look at some of your individual paintings, and maybe you can tell me what specific decisions confronted you in those paintings. Would that be all right with you?

Williams: That would be fine. But I think we must preface and announce that we speak to these points "after the fact."

Kramer: Right. I don't mean that decision-making is the basis of the painting. Obviously there are other things in the painting, and then to counteract the over-emphasis of decision-making maybe you can outline, to begin with, what it was you were trying to convey, what the main theme was and what decisions you had to make in the process.

Kramer: Here we are in your art studio-living-room, sitting in front of a painting that you did in 1959 ("The Three Women"). This is one of your early ones, but it's one that has always been a great favorite of mine. Maybe you can tell us something about what you were doing, what you had in mind with regard to this painting, and then get into the areas of this painting where you had to make particular decisions in regard to the nature of what you would or would not put in: or what critical points you may have been confronted with in the actual doing of the painting.

Williams: Well, with the male figures I had been working the idea of multiple image, without fracturing. That is several views of a figure in space, incorporated into the configuration of a figure. This was the basic idea, and I applied it to the female figure. I had done a couple of smaller versions. This is the first large painting I did.

Kramer: This canvas is about eight feet tall.

Williams: Yes. It is eight by six feet. When one is talking after the fact, one wonders how much he is concealing or forgetting, but let's try to reconstruct.

One of the matters of concern when I chose to paint three figures was a painting of three acrobats done by Walt Kuhn; I'd seen it years before in the old Whitney (down by the Clay Club in Greenwich Village). In 1939, when I attended the Art Students League, I had become very familiar with the Kuhn painting, and dearly loved it. I thought it was a great painting! To this day I think well of it. So the idea of three figures, rather than two, was something I wanted to do. This might be of interest—I have a suspicion that maybe those three figures from Kuhn's "Three Acrobats" created a standard for me, something that I had to match, but I did not consult a reproduction of his painting, you understand. Incidentally, while Kuhn's painting acted as a standard, my aim would be to efface his, were they to hang side by side.

Kramer: This is what you mentioned before—whatever painting you do is supposed to diminish, in a sense, or reduce what has gone before.

Williams: I know perfectly well that Rembrandt will still be there and deKooning will be there. (I admire deKooning no end. He is one of the great artists today, he and Bacon.) Yet my intent is to command the wall, wipe their work out of pictorial existence.

Kramer: That's your *self* coming to the fore. Right?

Williams: I intend to dominate. So we have the three figures—every time one deals with a form, the first one or two paintings are the primitives of that cycle. For example, the "guilty" series showed one-half of the man in the middle distance and the other half of the man close up. This was the primitive. But by the time I get to this ("The Three Women"), I find myself to be more sophisticated. I use a close-up on the left of this figure and then I use a close-up of the head on the right side, much more sophisticated. I think by this time the problem has been solved—it is now much easier to manipulate space and image on the canvas. By the way, the male figures did not accommodate themselves to the canvas as well as these female figures did.

Kramer: You mentioned something earlier—that this is accom-modating itself, of solving the problem within the confines, within certain limits. And, certainly the canvas is representing limits within which you have to solve what you are dealing with. Now my feeling is that with this painting ("The Three Women") you have done it admirably. Whatever new dimensions you have put into this painting, you have solved it so tremendously well that it is a multi-faceted painting. It stands as itself in terms of composition. It stands as itself in terms of emotional human aspects, and it lends itself to making art a confrontation, an experience, not just an event, not just something you are depicting photographically. When the viewer stands in front of this painting, it is an experience. And, so, I consider this particular painting extremely successful on all counts. That is how I measure a painting—when the artist solves the artistic problem; when he deals with the experiential problem; when he can solve the new dimensions he endeavors to incorporate. You have put these things all together and come up with an outstanding painting. I regard this as entirely successful!

Williams: There are certain things of interest about this painting. Somewhere along the line I got the idea that I was doing something that was unique to man—a male artist painting a female figure, in that I was trying to show a woman's view of herself. I've watched my wife observing the permutations of her body.

Kramer: It is very interesting that all these are female figures because they have breasts—nevertheless, the shape and contour of the face is male.

Williams: I meant to depict a middle-aged woman. I see what you are talking about, because of the baldness?

Kramer: Well, for example, you have no more than an eye, but the contour is such that it is female. There is no question about that. Here the contour . . . .

Williams: But it's a neutral face. It's the neutrality of middle-age, of the acceptance of middle-age. These two sides (on the left) have experienced themselves—they have experienced their sexual life; they have experienced living; they have experienced child bearing. The other sides look at themselves in a sort of terror, you know. That's a facet of the idea; that's the literary end of it.

You notice how scratched and scarified the surface is because I did this during the academic zenith of Abstract Expressionism, and process was the thing. It was the rage to paint, to scrape down, to repaint. Today, if I were to paint this, I think certainly I would paint it directly, whereas there I had to paint and wipe down, paint and wipe down. So you see, even though I was moving against Abstract Expressionism, I had to pay homage to it. Period vision has this kind of control.

As I look at it I see the strap, that vertical line, and the line on the floor. I remember agonizing as to whether or not to do it, whether or not its use would be banal.

Kramer: That was one of the decisions you had to make as far as this painting was concerned?

Williams: Correct. The fact is that I *needed* to do something like this. Diebenkorn used these straps all the time; and he wasn't alone. If I had to do this today I would run a scratch through there, or even a pencil line and it would turn the trick. At that time, however, this strap was identified with Diebenkorn, and the nature of influence is such that in certain instances it paralyzes one's imaginative faculties. There must be dozens of solutions, solving those areas, all of which I can see very clearly now. This kind of thing, I think, is affective on the painter's integrity, on his efforts to be his own man.

One time in California I laid up a couple of large shapes on a canvas, some abstract stuff, and they looked just fine. They seemed to represent a departure for me. Then I added two dots, for the painting demanded them, and, lo! It became a Miró! I rubbed the dots out and the painting looked incomplete. I put the two dots back and it was right, but it was a Miró. Talk about decision . . . .

Kramer: I know that one of your criteria is that it's "better to be a Hiram Williams of any kind than to be somebody else."

Williams: Than to ruin something by somebody else, maybe.

Kramer: Hiram, is that the only decision you had to make that "bugged" you in that painting?

Williams: You can see there the initial decision. This was the first time I had painted the women at a large scale, and I really didn't know what to do. And one of the elements involved was that I was horribly pressed for time—this actually was painted late in 1958. I signed it in January, 1959. You see, I painted it almost to completion in about two-and-one-half days. I had a grant for which I had agreed to do 25 paintings. I was to do five paintings six feet by twelve feet and to do 20 paintings six feet by eight feet. The pressure was really pretty strenuous.

Kramer: This is one of 20 paintings you did?

Williams: Twenty-five paintings!

Kramer: What has happened to the "guilty?"

Williams: One of the "guilty," a part of that project, went to the Museum of Modern Art. They each ended well placed.

I made several sketches. I began to draw some sort of horizontal image. I don't recall, Sol, what happened, but in a fraction of a second I changed my mind, and changed to standing figures. Somehow I recognized that I should approach the women much as I had the "guilty" male figures.

A problem was what to do back by the ground. In each case when I painted the "guilty" men, I had placed the figure in a sort of nowhere-land on a plane, topped by horizon lines. I was troubled by a lack of environmental definition in "The Three Women." I remember that friend Weismann, art historian, visited at the time I was fumbling. Weismann reassured me. When I signified that the idea of not having a descriptive interior bothered me and I didn't know what to do, he said, "You've already created a painted environment and that is as valid as anything in art—the idea of an environment of paint."

Kramer: That juxtaposition of the paint environment and the human image may do exactly what you want it to do on the canvas.

Williams: The fact is, the figure *is* the painting.

COLOR PLATES

Man of the Night (6′ x 4′)

Williams made the following remarks as he worked on the painting in his studio: "Before we are done we will have it, something right out of the Mafia. I am making his eyes have that Jack Palance menace. I flattened his neck to give him more of a 'bull-of-a-man' appearance. I cut in on his figure under the arm and on the leg to give the shape more intensity." (6/3/71)

Marching Figure (6′ x 4′)

The prototype of the "Marching Figure" image can be seen in the 1961 "Incubus" located in the National Collection of Fine Arts, Smithsonian Institution, Washington, D.C. The "Marching Figure" was in its early stages and had been brought back to Williams' studio for finishing work. Williams looked at it and assumed a drawl:

Before this day is done, this here painting is going to be transformed into
a first-rate painting; not a second, or third, or fourth-rate painting.

As he painted he started singing: "Let me whisper low. You can say what you want to. You can say whatever you care. Whisper love to me. Whisper words . . . hum . . . hum." All the while he was singing, Williams wiped the painting with a rag dipped in turpentine. "I want to get it loosened up, it's difficult to paint into a concise image. An amorphous shape is open, suggestive. I must do that one again." (6/3/71)

"He runs. Ant like. To where?" (9/28/71)

The Three Women (8′ x 6′)

". . .I was trying to show a woman's view of herself. I've watched my wife observing the permutations of her body." (7/15/71)

Small Chorus Line (60" x 40")

"When we walk down a street and see sidewalk magazine stands loaded with all the "girlie" magazines, you may have observed no one looks at the faces of the girls on the covers. The faces are lost to the eroticism of the bodies. Hence it was that I decided to make a chorus line without faces—'Playmate.'"

"I'd fashioned a considerable number of "Chorus Lines." One day I decided this was a figure that could be reduced below life size, therefore I did several — none of them particularly successful I'm afraid."

Trapped (3' x 3')

"It is a conceit of mine to focus a grin—a match for Rembrandt—as far as the revelation of human character is concerned." (1/15/70)

Wound (8' x 5') (intended to hang high on the wall)

(Williams marks across the skin surface.)

"Signs of damage—that is what it might be. . .Let's see if there are any more ways of adding to the slaughter." (5/12/70)

(Williams scratches random lines across the canvas.)

"Got to make it look as if some maniacal person had been fooling around, dabbling—dabbling to satisfy his appetite." (5/13/70)

"Let the strings dangle. They add a dimension to it, I think. If I bind something with wire or rope, twine, or what have you, this is the result: the after effect of violence."

(While using spray cans of paint Williams talks.)

"It is strange how things come to one. It is not like saying I am going to do thus and so and then do it. But I think after I did this first panel it was a whole lot easier to get the epidermal tissue effect on the second panel. One must separate muscle from muscle, and create white fatty tissue. It is something beautiful, isn't it."

"One can overdo this savagery, and if so it then becomes melodramatic and unbelievable." (5/13/70)

Forksville Mountain (3'6" x 5')

"I paint the mountain so that it is without season. I want you to think of this as a mountain rather than it being Spring or Autumn.

"This is at the edge of the valley. I lived forty miles back down the valley. Avonell's folks had a farm on the plateau atop this mountain. She lived near Estella, Pennsylvania.

"I painted the mountain and depicted a spot of light laving its top, a leveled off place. I think of Forksville Mountain as a kind of burned mountain." (7/15/71)

Man Confronting Himself (8′ x 6′)

"Came upon the idea of 'jittering man' some time back (or it came upon me—). I mean to paint 'Jittering Crowds' and so forth, but meantime painted this. I depict the nude back of the figure moving in upon the confronting and nervous man. Each of us confronts the beast in ourselves."

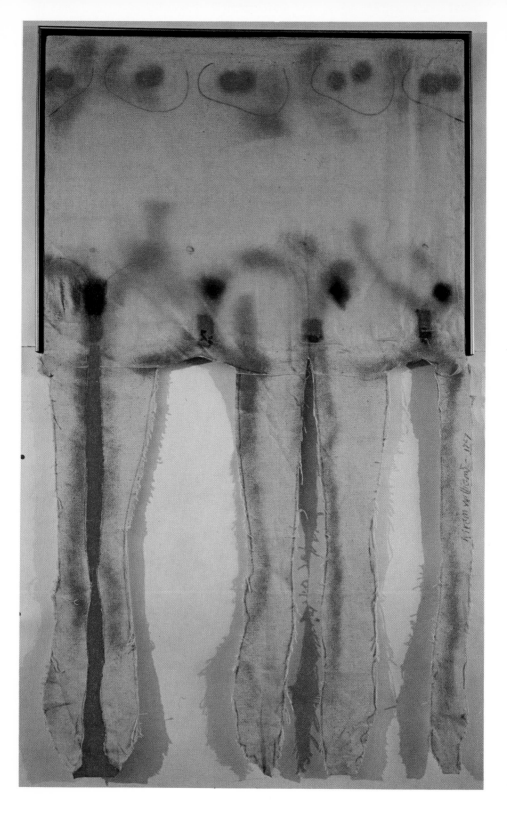

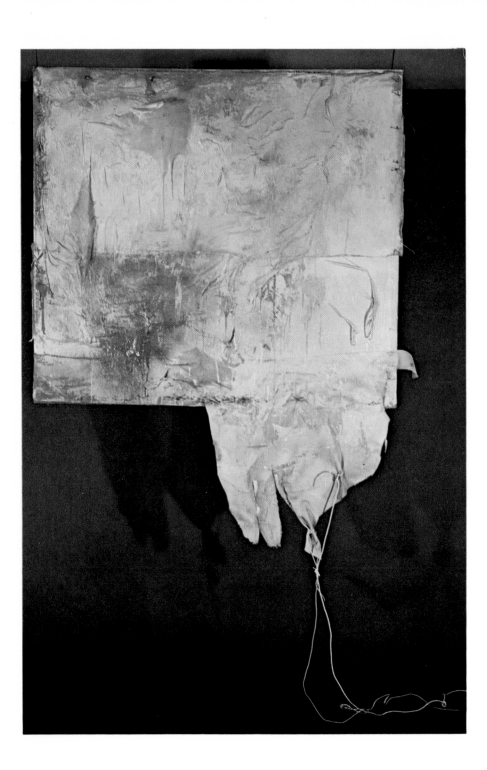

Interview

Williams' Dining Room and Living Room
31 August 1971

Kramer: Bill, you were asking why Hiram had concentrated on noses. Hiram, would you care to pursue that?

Williams: I have the notion that art, as art, often tells the artist of himself. Remember, I said that when I got in what seemed an obsessive state about roads (doing roads in Texas), after I'd done a number of them I woke up one day and realized I had driven across the country two and a half times prior to adopting the theme. I had been seeing only roads. I told you the story of the exhibition in Chicago at the Kovler Gallery and of the two overly-cultivated men in mod clothes who came up to me. They pointed to the walls which were full of double mouths that I had been painting—no eyes, just teeth and mouths. And one of the men said, "Why your obsession with mouths?" And the reason hit me! I pulled out my dental plate and waved it in their faces. The pair staggered away. And it was true—I had at that moment had the insight—I had been going through extensive dental work. I knew I was concentrating on mouths, of course, but I had seen the subject purely as idea—as how to simulate a laugh—to say ha, ha; ha, ha. Or have two mouths to say ha, ha; ha, ha. Lead the viewer to make the mouth laugh. But there was more to it than that. The reason for inception of the idea, I think, was because I had been having dental work! Now this is not always the case, but can likely as not be the case. So I did mouths, and then the next obvious thing, I began to do crowds of mouths as well as single heads. I think pretty much as an intellectual notion, I began to use one eye because I began to have a notion of "one"—to take one feature in a head and through suggestion convey the entire personality of the entire head. And I moved toward eyes after I had done so many mouths that I became repetitious. I did silhouettes of crowds of heads and then one or two eyes to carry the entire crowd. Sometimes I'd have two heads against each other to make a single configuration—have one eye carry the two heads—or sometimes have obviously two heads but place one eye in one head and place the opposite eye in the other head.

The first time I did a nose I had been doing cheeks and a mouth; sometimes two cheeks and a mouth; sometimes four cheeks and a mouth, one above the other; sometimes just one cheek and the corners. Then one day I drew a nose, and nothing else. And I knew I had found something. I was excited enough to drive the nine or ten miles to friend Hollis Holbrook's to share my discovery.

Kramer: Let me go back to eyes for a moment—this is the beginning of your avenue of human encounter; not only a beginning but a most significant one, Hiram. Just as infants need to be held, they require skin contact. They also require eye contact—they must have mothers looking at them, and be able to look into mother's eyes.

Williams: I know that if I stare at a stranger, even a second or two longer than in a usual encounter, and if one of us doesn't lower our eyes there is trouble potential there. I understand that. True of two gorillas encountering one another, too.

Kramer: With children, if their eye-to-eye contact is a normal development, they are able to look at other people and express a great deal. In that sense, the phrase, "The eyes are windows of the soul," has great validity. But what happens in the development of most people is at one point or another they break off contact with their mothers; either the mother breaks off contact (sometimes the mother can't tolerate the intensity of that feeling) or the children get unhappy with their mothers and stop looking. As soon as they stop looking, they begin imagining their relationship with their mother. They never have it in reality. And from that point onward a particular characterological pattern of use of the eyes becomes set. Eyes are extremely interesting, especially what people do with them. The reason I have gone on about this explanation is because I would like to know what it is about individual features of the face that excites and attracts you? I don't believe you would paint and emphasize mouths or eyes or noses without some strong awareness of what they express What of what they express. What meaning do they have for you?

Williams: Perhaps I can articulate this, Sol. The interesting thing—and I didn't know this when I took the drawing out to Hollis, but later as I began to put in collage noses in simple contoured heads—there was a certain striking relationship of description and formality. The photographic reproduction with the hand-drawn contour line made for a certain sensation because of contrast. When I create an image, I am not emblemizing or making a metaphor; my intent is to literally place a man there. I am not interested in art questions—how does a red look beside a green and that sort of thing. I've gone through a phase of this, but I've never really been caught up. Somehow to give a sense of *us* there on the canvas—and the nose does it! That is what is astonishing to me, whereas the eye and the mouth are features we think of as windows to the personality, I found the nose gave a sense of "thereness"—of somebody there. Who? I don't know! But somebody. And that's what has fascinated me with the nose as image.

Kramer: We look at faces in their total expressiveness, using eyes, nose, mouth, cheeks, and musculature of the face, we normally think of the total expression as conveying a particular feeling or an aspect of the individual. But you are saying, if I hear you right, that individual elements of the face also convey the *totality*!

Williams: Right. I have shown these noses to many lay people, to my relatives, etc., and they do not miss eyes or mouths. "Hiram, that's a portrait of you," they will tell me. Or they will recognize somebody. "Is that so and so?" They are supplying the entire phiz, features and character.

Kramer: In other words, people are much more perceptive about individual and isolated communications or reflections of the human personality.

Williams: And also more *imaginative* than we give them credit. From a little outline and a nose, which is flat to boot and illusionistic, they supply the whole mask, everything. And what is interesting is that this is a "fool the mind," not a "fool the eye" thing—a "fool the mind" thing because they do it and are not aware of it. They are not missing anything because in their minds nothing is missing.

Kramer: In other words, all the parts of the face are so fully integrated that whatever the face expresses must be in each part.

Williams: Given a clue, we supply that which is missing. A gestalt is made of a fragment of visual description.

Kramer: Then if you are really observant and you know mouths, or you know eyes, you can almost sense the rest of the individual from that one part. And another thing I hear you saying is that most people, apart from artists, are aware of the expressiveness of the features of the face. Just as we ordinarily know our friends, not only from the look of their faces, but if you can't see a friend's face, if you see him walking even from the back side, as Van Gogh depicted so knowingly, you recognize the gait of his walk, the way he ambles along, the way he energetically walks—you recognize "walks." You come to recognize friends, people that are close to you, from very small details.

Williams: Sol, what would you say to this? I painted somebody completely, frontally, with the nose, mouth and entire features. Then I put one of the heads with nothing but the collaged nose beside the completed head. And the sense of reality of somebody there was markedly stronger in the collaged nose than in the pretty well described portrait. Once, while I had my seminar here at the house, I put up one of the collaged noses, and had one of my students, who had a head relative in size, stand by the collage. And we all looked to see which was the realer. And, of course, the collaged nose was the realer. This is no news to a portrait artist. If you have the model stand beside the portrait and ask people to look at them both, they will utterly ignore the model, beyond reference from the portrait to the model, to see if the portrait is accurate. The reality exists not in the model, which is real flesh and blood, but in the portrait.

Kramer: That excites me, Hiram! I'm writing a paper right now, and one of the things I'm writing about is the reaction of animals, such as birds, to what are termed *supernormal objects* in ethology. For example, if a Ringed Plover is brooding and you fashion a dummy wooden egg (the Plover's natural egg is light brown with dark brown spots) and place it in the nest of a brooding bird, it will also brood it. But if you exaggerate the size of the spots, and instead of making them brown you make them black so that they contrast even more with a painted white background, and place this painted wooden egg alongside the nest of the Ringed Plover, the Ringed Plover will get off its own natural eggs in the nest and over to the dummy egg and sit down on that! It (the wooden egg) is much more attractive for releasing its brooding behavior than its own natural egg. Ethologists can exaggerate one or two key stimuli which convey a message to an animal. And not only that, the animals react to the . . .

Williams: Now you suppose that this is one of the reasons that art in the matter of human affairs has been successful up to now? It's a dumb show! Art always has been an illusionistic dumb show.

Kramer: We call these key stimuli—the spots on the egg or the shape of the egg—"releasers." They release behavior and feelings. For example, a male Stickleback in its nesting territory will attack anything with a red belly. You can put a normal looking dummy that looks exactly like a Stickleback, but without the red belly, and it doesn't bother to attack it. You take something that is gross, that is bizarre, that doesn't even look like a Stickleback, but you put a red belly on it and ZOOM! It immediately attacks it! You might say this is a primitive form of abstraction, isn't it! It is a kind of abstraction in that they can abstract the key quality which represents the entire object. Now my students always laugh when I show them these sketches of animals reacting to fake stimuli, but then I talk to them about such things as the exaggerated stimuli in the *Playboy* magazine models (big breasts, long legs and big asses) and how excited they get. Or, girls look at a Hollywood movie magazine of exaggerated masculinity objects, and I ask, "What are you getting so excited about, you are just looking at pieces of paper? In real life you have the real stuff around you." I'm usually talking to a class of a hundred, with boys and girls alongside each other. The real live stuff within reach hardly excites them, but they see paper models, and they go completely crazy. You can almost hear them swoon.

Williams: And, of course, Plato knew this with his "shadows on the wall" being realer than reality.

Kramer: You know, what brought this on was your comparison of a real live model and the painting; that people are more attracted to the painting than they are to the flesh and blood model.

Williams: That's right, they will look at the flesh and blood model in a most cursory way. I mean there is no way to stress their observation of the model beyond a comparison with the important thing, which is the dummy, the replication or whatever you want to call it.

Kramer: Why is that? How do you as an artist react to all this?

Williams: I'm just wondering if we aren't talking about the same thing—the Stickleback fish gets the red thing and he supplies the rest imaginatively.

Kramer: We don't know that he supplies the rest; he reacts to the releasers.

Williams: Well, I'm just suggesting that, because, for example, I don't think that is a notable hunk of art right there, but when we look at that we don't say, where are her eyes, her nose? We *know* that is a very sexy girl!

Kramer: Right!

Williams: We even know she is pretty; we understand that she has a hairdo from the thirties. We know a hell of a lot about her.

Stephens: Does the German Expressionism of the 1920s influence you?

Williams: Oh no, because I've never liked it; it is utterly non-formal. This work is one of the things I came to on my own, most decidedly. I began to move in Texas toward a contour, a silhouette of figurative images. I moved toward silhouette because I was searching for images, unfamiliar outlines so to speak, or familiar outlines that could still carry the freight of new expression. While dealing with neophytes in drawing, I found out that beginning draftsmen deal in contour. If one gave them charcoal they would never take the flat of their crayon and use it broadside. They use the point. Maybe this is because they have been conditioned to use pencils all of their lives. In any event, they tend to use outline. Somehow our perception is such that our eye picks up a contour. We recognize the world through contour. What would I have if I supplied a nose without the outline of a head? I don't know whether it is the nose that is giving reality or the outline. I think they have to be in combination. I think just the silhouette itself wouldn't suffice. I don't think enough would be supplied the viewer. There would be an awareness of this being the outline of a head as opposed to the comprehension people have of the whole visage when a collage nose is supplied.

Kramer: This comes close to what ethologists call "key stimuli." In other words, if you looked at a nose you might not be aware that it was a nose, but when you place it within the outline (even though the rest of the face is absolutely featureless, it is blank) those two characteristics or stimuli are sufficient to call attention to the fact that this is a human being. Once the idea of a human being is accepted, then the nose fits into it and completes it; you know what goes with a particular nose and a particular shape of a head; you fill in the rest of the character of the individual from your deep unconscious experience. Doesn't every viewer use unconscious knowledge of what human beings are like when he or she reacts to a painting?

Williams: Suppose I had the outline of the head we are looking at and instead of a human nose I drew a hog snoot. I bet you, because of the outline, it would be read as human. It would lose, of course. It would gain only what a caricature gains. I think it would be caricature. The outline is conveying the sense that here is a human, but I think the psychological sense of somebody being there is carried by the neutrality of a *human* nose; furthermore, one not expressive of individualized character.

Kramer: That reminds me of another aspect. Have you ever seen the cartoons of pet owners and their animals? There are many of those where the face of the owner is just like the animal; so that, in a sense, the cartoonist has given animal characteristics to the human; and in spite of the fact that they are animal characteristics, you recognize them as being *potentially* human characteristics. Sometimes a human being can exaggerate certain animal aspects to such an extent that they have almost a fusion of human and animal characteristics. You accept them as human, with their animal-like characteristics, distortions, or idiosyncracies.

In certain types of therapy, people sometimes feel that their own noses are snout-like, pig-like. Now that shouldn't be surprising because we, as mammals, at one time made great use of our noses. That is a sensory mechanism, by the way, which we hardly employ as adults, although children are very sensitive (in a positive way) to body odors. As primates we primarily employ our eyes, but we do have what we call a "smelling" brain. And, in infancy and childhood smell is extremely important: the smell of people close to us; the smell of the beds of our parents; the smell of their bodies, all are exciting. Most people lose that as they develop, and we become visual people. We may, or may not, become touch people. Very often we lose a lot of our sense of touch. It seems as if the eyes take over. But the other characteristics are still there and can be developed. Now, in some individuals, perhaps the smelling quality of the nose has not receded into the background. Perhaps it's there and that's what people sense when they look at a particular kind of nose—when they look at an individual and say, yes, well that *is* snout-like. In other words, if you are saying that the people who view these things react and supply the material then I wonder where they get that information if not from their own deep unconscious, and their deep knowledge of many other features of human beings?

Don't your paintings affirm some aspect of their being, some aspect of knowledge which in ordinary discourse nobody talks about, but is present?

Williams: Bill and I have talked of this. I have wondered if our minds (I'll use the simile of a computer) have memory banks and so forth; and if the nature of the mind is to take imagery (information) and generalize it and store it away. For example, we say that so and so has painted a picture that has a "universal image." And we look at another painting and say that someone has particularized too much, it is not universal. What is universal? It must be an image that somehow aligns itself with the nature of the generalization that is in our memory banks. Would you buy that? Because I have a sense that this is what I am trying to do, what my images tap. As a matter of fact, when somebody says, "Is that a portrait of you," I feel a bit as if I missed the boat, because what I would like them to feel is that somehow they have encountered this person. They can't recall where and when. They can't pin down the personality, but they have met him. I wish the viewer to feel he's encountered the personality in real life at the moment he encounters the image.

Kramer: I suspect what you say is true. Deep in the knowledge of many people are stores of information they ordinarily do not use, yet at a moment's notice—when you present one of your paintings to them—they draw on this store of information. And they do it instantly.

Williams: There are stores of information not used, but doesn't that lead to this. Maybe they are using such information constantly, while quite unaware. For example, when I met you I don't think for a moment that I had met you for the first time. I had met you before in others who bear a general likeness to Sol Kramer. And when you met me, I don't think I was startling to you. And I don't think I have startled you since.

Kramer: What is exciting is that when we meet *any* face—any individual—it seldom startles us. We can meet the most grotesque individual and not be startled. We accept that as an aspect of humanity, as an aspect of mankind.

Williams: But isn't it often because we have met them before? Maybe not in real life, but well, because we have experienced daVinci's fellows, the ones with the wattled noses and the like. I, for example, one day was in a restaurant in New York, and saw a restauranteur reading a paper while standing against the wall. And I suddenly realized what a nose he had! He had a nose that looked like four or five enormous potatoes attached to one another. Now, whether it was New York where anything strange can be seen, or whether somehow daVinci had prepared me, I can't say. Somehow I had been prepared. Somehow, I had met him before, and I was not shocked.

Kramer: What lies behind that? I don't think it is only art. I don't think it is only the fact that . . . .

Williams: I think this says something about what I've been doing—when talking about human beings in art, and getting at this thing we call truth, reality, it is as if I want to put an image there that is known to all. Yet in every aspect it is strange. In the use of a nose rather than the entire mask, there is a strangeness in that kind of image. But in creating this strangeness I am also trying to capture the aspects of that head most familiar to the viewer, in order to intrigue him and give him emotional contact with it.

Kramer: If I hear you, Hiram, what you are saying is that what we call grotesque, or idiosyncratic, or unusual (in human expression, in human communication, in human countenance, in human posture, in human movement, in human behavior), by the mere fact that it is an aspect of being human, it is not that grotesque. That is the part we are familiar with—all these idiosyncratic behaviors and modifications of man that are possible in this world. Somehow that is an aspect of man's humanity, that he can appear in so many different guises, and we somehow recognize the basic humanness underneath all the modifications of man.

Williams: Finally, I want you to encounter yourself when you look at one of my drawings.

Kramer: Hiram, I want to ask one more question, or at least make a comment about my own reaction to these portraits. I personally consider some of them more successful than others, and I want to explore this with you. For instance, I think this is a successful one—with the silver and the pink body, and then the nose in a sort of charcoal color with a silver shadow on the pink. I know you have said you are not interested in the painting; you said earlier you are not interested in combinations of red, yellow and green, composition, and the complementarity of colors. Yet there is something about a painting which is successful because it conveys more than an essential truth. Writings, literary works contain essential truths.

Some scientific statements contain essential truths. So the question arises, what differentiates a painting as a conveyor of essential truth from these other conveyors of essential truth? Is that a fair question? Let me interpose a further comment before I ask you to answer this. What conveys an artistic essential truth is not only that you have a basic idea which you want to get across—whatever that may be—and you put it together in such a way that it not only communicates the idea, but artistically it has its own sense of validity, of balance, call it composition, or what you may. These are trite words, but nevertheless, they convey that somehow within the frame of the canvas you solve a certain problem "artistically," as well as communicate some essential truth that you feel as a person. Does what I have said ring a bell? I'd like you to comment because sometimes I feel that you are imbued with an essential truth, that you are concentrating on essential truths, but artistically you have not yet put the whole thing together. Some of your paintings strike me as preliminary steps to what is to come. Does that ring a bell with you?

Williams: The one man that I've met in my career, in the sense that our ships passed in the night, is T. S. Eliot. I happened to have had the pardonable privilege of having overheard him say once in response to the question, "Mr. Eliot, which do you prefer, some kind of pentameter, some kind of hexameter," (something like this) and Mr. Eliot, who was extremely old at the time replied, "Young man, I never think of those things. I just write my verse until it seems right to me." And, I think there is something like that involved in my work. What seems right can vary with the creator from time to time. When I sign a painting or drawing, obviously it seems right to me at the moment. Then the next day I may tear up the whole darn thing because it has turned sour. What might seem wrong to me is an awareness that I have become mannered or repetitious. Or there is a flaw in the work. I may have recognized the functioning in the paint and material isn't in support of my idea. And at that point, it must go, be destroyed, if it is beyond correction.

Kramer: That's well put. I like that. That's what I'm getting at. Because, somehow, many of your paintings convey the idea that the way you put things together is just the right, and economic, support for your theme.

Williams: I can paint a bad painting and not know that I've done so. I think I have a heck of a good eye, a critical eye, for student painting and other painting. One of the reasons, as I tell them, is that I am outside their painting and emotionally uninvolved beyond my interest in them as students, in their growth. I also tell them that when it comes to this, I am no different than they are—I can make a miserable botch of it and not realize I have until later. I do say this, one of the differences between them and me is that I am liable to wake up faster than they might because I have more reference in my previous work. I think part of what we are doing is training art students to step back, take a look at what they are doing, and achieve an objective state of mind, which is hard to do. It is a learned behavior. I don't know whether I've told you this before, but one of the problems with painting is that when one picks up and applies a brush, one moves into a mental fog. Have I discussed this with you? You can try it yourself. You'll find out that one can be the rational man, looking at his work, and one can say to himself, "I am going to paint a red line, just so." The canvas is touched with the red-tipped brush, and at that point one will find the hand is going in just the opposite direction, putting the red somewhere else than where planned. That is "fog." Now, how to manipulate, how to handle yourself under this condition is part of the problem. For example, when I instruct a student in some aspect, I hardly ever expect him to apply what I have just taught him. It may be days, hours, or months before he will one day wake up and say to himself, "My God, this is what Williams meant." One of the problems of teaching art is that it is seldom taught straight away.

Kramer: Why do you say that so strongly?

Williams: As an art teacher, I live with this frustration.

Kramer: What is it that has to take place in order for art to develop and to grow? You are saying that the cognitive, or simply the intellectual knowledge of something, is not adequate. What is it you are hoping will develop in your students?

Williams: The subconscious, or whatever other levels of mind get into play before they are able to handle it.

Kramer: So a part of art instruction is the freeing of the subconscious?

Williams: If it is any instruction at all, it has to take into account this unknown factor.

Kramer: So, would you say that every good art teacher is aware of this element?

Williams: I can't see how he could teach art without having a sense for it.

Kramer: You are saying, then, that no matter what he is saying on a cognitive level, or a technical level, the teacher is always aware that the student must contribute his free-flowing subconscious which he utilizes or which manipulates him. That's interesting. In a sense, the extreme mutual interest we often have in human beings from the psychiatric-psychoanalytic subconscious realm and the artistic awareness of the subconscious realm meet at this point. Remember that time we had you and Hollis over to the Psychiatry Department talking at Grand Rounds? That was one of the most successful Grand Rounds we ever had! Because the psychiatrists realized, perhaps for the first time—and that's what I hoped they would—that the artist has as much an intuitive sense of the subconscious realm as they have. The artist reads people from the very elements we have been talking about—a nose, an eye, the lips, the sexiness, the form, the shape, etc.—just as they are reading what they call "body language" and non-verbal communication. Apart from what is said, every person communicates something else. That session you and Hollis had with the Psychiatry Department was very successful. A number of psychiatrists, residents and others, told me how much they enjoyed it.

Stephens: You want a student to free himself so he can bring forth things from the subconscious, but what keeps this from being nothing more than sheer expression, apart from what one knows about formality?

Williams: Because I think that is where the idea in art comes into being. Idea becomes a kind of container, or a kind of delimiting point, so that the impulse to do things can somehow be controlled. In the dialogue between the painter and the canvas, via the medium, you are in a sense telling it and it is busy telling you. It can tell you to do things that are completely erroneous, of course. One must somehow be able to govern in the haze-like state he is in ; there must be some kind of control so that he doesn't behave in an utterly random way. This is one of the reasons a "Sunday Painter," who has had a considerable experience looking at art and what not—one of the reasons his work will end up as a hodge-podge of style. He is not consciously imitating Van Gogh, he is being fed Van Gogh. He makes another mark and it suggests Seurat. So suddenly he becomes a "Pointillist." And he is "Pointillizing" away, and his brush stoke flattens and suddenly he becomes a Cézanne, and pretty soon we have a God-awful mess. Friends now come along and say how creative this person is, he uses all kinds of brush stokes, while the fact is that he has been completely out of control all of the time.

Kramer: Hiram, what you are saying, if I hear you right, is that if the material does flow freely from the subconscious, then whatever comes out will have some sort of integrity of its own. It won't be a hodge-podge. The depth level of the artist has an integrity of its own.

Williams: But it won't necessarily be a consistent thing. For example, if we are talking about style and one has absorbed somebody's style, the influence becomes apparent. Part of what the teacher does is to teach the student recognition of styles, so he can eliminate influence from his own work. It could be that he has followed a form pattern that happens to be one that Miró has thoroughly explored. I know this is a pattern that he wouldn't have done if he hadn't known Miró, because very few of them have the peculiar "genius" of Miró. So what I suspect is that the information he has is being fed him, and he is creating a Miró unwittingly. He either wakes up to it, or he doesn't wake up to it on his own. The good teacher will make certain that he wakes up to the influence.

Kramer: I wonder how much of that is related to what happens to people who learn to write the Palmer Method. We have all started off in the Palmer Method or some other formalized type of writing—the so-called ideal which is usually not very expressive of the personality. I have known people in their thirties, forties and fifties who are still writing that way. On the other hand, I think most individuals incorporate some aspect of their own personality in writing, and no matter how they start off their writing becomes their own. It is an expression of themselves. Isn't this similar to what takes place in art? What I'm saying is that it wouldn't hurt if you started off copying, in fact this is the business of learning through copying. So what if you start with Van Gogh or you start with Miró, as long as you only use that as a beginning; and then allow your own expressive need to come through.

Williams: We say "growing out of influence"—as Van Gogh grew out of Impressionism.

Kramer: Right.

Williams: But some never make it.

Stephens: What are you laughing about?

Williams: I was thinking about one's own personality. I sometimes wish I could really use the Palmer Method, because my writing seems to have such notable lack of character. Any kind of good properties . . . .

Kramer: I'm not so sure about that. Actually, graphologists are awfully good at deciphering. They can tell as much from handwriting as the psychiatrists can tell from hours and hours, or even years of therapy. Every handwriting, however consciously stylized, contains elements of unconscious expression.

Williams: God knows what handwriting experts think of us—most painters I know are deplorable penmen. I get letters from art friends, and they write slanting one direction, than a few lines later on slanting the other direction. The letters gain strength, and then they become weaker than hell, on and on.

Kramer: Are their paintings the same way?

Williams: No, but I don't know of any good artist that can paint a sign. Because when we letter, we draw letters. Absolutely all my life I've been plagued by some Woman's Club member or somebody similar wanting me to make a damn sign, and I have to dodge. I can make a sign under duress, but these are terrible signs. The layout can be great, but the actual work—because I draw letters, or I paint letters—I can't conceivably do what a sign painter does. If I find a painter that can make good signs, I'll show you a bad artist, almost always. Well, you would think this hand has been using paint brushes for thirty years. It ought to be able to do a sign, but that is not so.

Kramer: Hiram, the last time we talked about your paintings we discussed this one ("The Three Women") with the three almost asexual figures that you did in 1959. And you mentioned a "moment of decision" when you have to decide exactly what you are going to do in a painting; whether you are going to put something in or not. Every painting, you said, has some moment of decision, and I wonder whether you would look around this living room at some other paintings on the wall, and indicate what particular decision had to be made with regard to the completion or even the continuation or the initiation of a painting. I like this concept of "decision."

Williams: There are a couple of controls needful for the creation of my art. One control is the *idea,* which usually has to do with the metaphorical realization of an image drawn out of nature, usually human. And, the other is the *picture plane.* I am working in terms, then, of the real world, an idea drawn out of the real world. And the pictorial world, which has as a common denominator the plane, the picture plane. To belabor a truism, we are the result of our experience. I grew, after World War II, through 12 years of "abstract expressionism." The fact is, my creative ambience was pervaded by the sensibility of that movement, its mannerisms, its techniques, and so forth. For example, the painting of "The Three Women" has a "processed surface," which means I painted, scrubbed, and changed. You will notice there is a ghost on the shoulder of the right figure that strikes through from an underpainting that was painted over. There is no way a painter can avoid what we call period vision. The intent, when we process a painting, is to make it grow out of the canvas. Now this is, of course, an impossibility in the sense that painting is imagery imposed upon a surface. But the feeling of the picture, the sensation of it, must be that it grew out of the surface. I do a great deal of process painting to this day because of my conditioning. In a sense, I think much of my work would be better in respects if I painted directly, which I can do. But somehow if I don't process, I feel a lack of validity. I must immerse myself in what I think is a disgusting practice in painting—the practice of processing.

Kramer: I wasn't aware Hiram, that you process your paintings, but I am aware that you have a sort of abstract background. The thing I like about your paintings is that they are successful both as figure paintings and as abstracts. I feel that your best paintings are those that combine these two elements. That is, they are not only paintings of the human figure which I prefer to abstracts, not that I don't like abstracts—I do. I have some in my own living room, and I enjoy their movement and vitality, but you seem to have combined concern with the human condition with an imposition, a superposition, of an abstract quality. So one can look at the painting as an abstract, and one can look at it as a human figure.

Williams: What you have just said is an approach of which I am utterly aware. I am dealing in these two ways all the time, in terms of formal, abstract, pictorial behavior and vision, and in terms of theme and apparition drawn out of the phenomenal world. There was a fine painter named Lee Gatch who did semi-abstractions. He died recently, of old age, I think. Lee Gatch was quoted several years ago as saying, "In dealing with the painting, descriptive passages must yield to formal solutions, should doubt as to solution arise." Now this is not true in my case, but the awareness that Gatch had was never lost on me; and I can't imagine a painting escaping my studio that couldn't be measured in formal terms. Paintings must function formally!

Kramer: Then you view a painting as humanities people sometimes depreciate the sciences for being too mechanistic. You have a respect for the formal but you don't want the formal to pervade the work, so that the formality alone is felt. You want the essential message to come through, together with the formality. That makes for a successful work as far as your own endeavors are concerned because you have several concerns, as you voiced them to me. On the one hand, you want the person not only to view the painting, but also to feel the painting as an experience. And then you want the painting to confront the person. You want him to confront what is in the painting, and in himself. Then you want to convey the fact that you are dealing with the human condition. In your own terms, a successful painting would be one that includes all these elements and successfully puts them together. Then you could look at the painting and say: "That's it!"

Williams: I describe to my students what this formal business means; of course, there are all sorts of approaches and devices to elicit a formal appearance. But I use Norman Rockwell's illustration of grandma and grandchild saying grace in a restaurant. There are a couple of seated truck drivers with their hats in their hands. It's fine illustration. It is doing just that, showing grandma shaming the truck drivers by saying grace—innocence over brute strength, etc. But it doesn't achieve the attitude of art for this very reason. The grandma's pocketbook can be on the floor. The truck drivers could wear shirts of any color. They could have any type of work clothes. Grandma could have any style grandma clothes; grandma could be shifted. The illustrator's intent is to give the viewer the feeling that grandma came in, sat down, and soon shamed these brutish men. Grandma and the grandson will leave, and the men will be better off for having encountered innocence. Now there is a comparable painting by a Mister Whistler (for whom I have no great brief). Nevertheless, he did understand formality, and he painted "Whistler's Mother,"—mother sitting in a chair, under a picture on the wall. We are all familiar with it. Now I challenge you or anyone else to change a thing in that painting and not change the picture. In fact it can't be done. Move the figure, or move the chair to one side or the other, up or down, and we will have a radically changed painting; whereas we could move grandma anywhere in Rockwell's painting and not have harmed the content of the painting in the least.

Kramer: Now you are geting to the subject I have been struggling with in viewing your works, namely that there is nothing wrong with a painting conveying an idea—the fact that a painting conveys some essential truth can often contribute to its validity. But the conveying of a cognitive or intellectual something is not sufficent for a work of art.

Williams: Correct.

Kramer: If it only conveys an idea, then it's illustration, it is not art. That's what I sense myself. And you have put into words what I sense as a layman. I've always had a feeling, although I'm not an artist, that I'm able to look at art works and know what's good, because I have a sense of the extent to which the artist has put these two elements of his work together. If I only get the intellectual message, it's a message, not a painting.

Williams: Here is where Dali falls apart.

Kramer: What I was hoping to extract from you is just this conception (which I find interesting): that the way you put together the material artistically, and what you are attempting to convey (which is something deeply important to you on the human level) must lock— must fit together. Your paintings are successful to the extent that these two things happen. Those of your paintings that give satisfaction are those which satisfy all the endeavors you feel should go into a good painting—that is as you conceive them and work them out. If you are able to put all these things together, then you are satisfied.

Williams: You must understand, in my painting the formality must come out of the image. For example, in this "Chorus Line" the nipples are nipples. But in a row, and as I paint them, I am aware of them as tension points. Now, permit me to vary our discussion. We have paintings of "confrontation." As I stand here, Sol, directly before you, here, of course, I am. May I remind you that the human figure is a notably informal sort of affair unless it is actually confronted head on, straight away. As I've said, art is not a picturing of experience, but it *is* the experience, an altogether different thing. The Norman Rockwell painting is a *picturing* of experience and the Whistler *is* the experience. If I confront you head on we are utterly formal. It is a direct confrontation, and that is where the experience lies. But the minute I move my head, you've got to move in on me in order to read me. This is when descriptive art can become endangered pictorially because I can too quickly begin to describe through my picture something that happens in the world, non-art. So now we are moving into an area where a painting can be a picturing of an *event*. One must read into the "Chorus Line" and read the undulating bellies, read the description, the formalities, the same as in a Pollock painting. The viewer must read into the Pollock, into the maze. Points and planes must keep a surface tension. And if the painter relaxes so that somehow the painting begins to have less presence in terms of its parts, the painting begins to fall apart, it slackens and becomes non-formal at that point. Perhaps at that point it becomes of the real world rather than the pictorial one; because we don't see the real world as shapes functioning in tension.

When I speak of confrontation I speak of this image (pointing to the outline forming the big shape in the "Head") as being the *hero*. Here the *hero*, an outline of a figure, and inside the outline, shapes behave. Here is *event*. So, first we viewers are engaged in *confrontation* with the *hero*, and then the shapes behaving, the *event*. If I can get this information across to the student—that we paint in terms of *confrontation*, or we paint in terms of *event*—some of his confusion is abated.

Kramer: That's the most powerful statement about painting I have ever heard. I was startled by it when you mentioned that last time, because it taught me something I never knew.

Williams: Did I mention it? I had forgotten that I had.

Kramer: I never thought about painting in those terms—in that particular way, but I realized that it had the ring of validity. In other words, when the artist is simply *describing* an "event," that falls in the category of an illustration. But when the viewer is "confronted," and experiences something at a deep level of his psyche, then art becomes what you claim: art is experience. If someone paints with either of those two points, or two positions, in mind, completely different paintings will be produced. One can't possibly start out with your sense of what the goal is and produce the same painting as somebody that is going to illustrate an event. That is an enormous difference, isn't it?

As you were talking about that, I thought of something in a completely different field, and yet the same principle applies. I was talking to a college chaplain, and he was telling me his problems of getting students these days to be interested in spiritual and religious themes. I started telling him what I knew about patients' experiences with LSD psychotherapy, and how almost to a person, if they remained in LSD psychotherapy long enough, they would have mystical, cosmic, or religious experiences. It didn't matter who they were or how atheistic they were, they had these experiences. "You know," he told me, "*you* taught me a lesson about religion that I had not even known." "I would never have learned it from religion," I replied. I told him that I thought the failure of religion today is due to the fact that it has become a belief system. You believe in religion, you don't experience mystical, magical, cosmic events. As a matter of fact, religion arose from the mystical experiences of other people, that's what gave rise to religion. Today, if somebody says he has experienced something mystical, the church brands him a heretic, instead of saying, "Marvelous, you have had a religious experience." Oh no, you must now subvert your own mystical experience, and substitute a belief system in its place. Isn't that equivalent to what you are talking about in art?

Williams: Sol, have you gone to the colored churches around here? Would you accept an invitation and go with me to the Arredondo Church? An interesting phenomena of these churches is that everybody participates. I am invariably asked to come up and sit with the deacons because I am their white friend. We go to this church on the order of once a month or every six weeks.

Kramer: I'd like to go with you.

Williams: You'd be welcomed generously. They are truly happy. They have a program. Back in this little country church, they send out a program with a black and white handclasp on it. They are doing their damnedest to teach brotherly love. And, my God, everyone of them are people who are our janitors, and people who are being kicked around. You know how they are treated—like non-persons. And yet, there they are. It is not only astonishing, it is one of the most human things. Oh, I don't know, the variety of phenomena that occurs in largeness-of-spirit and naturalness, unselfconscious behavior. They have just gotten through a week of "sing meets" where their choirs meet and rotate through the churches in the evenings, and then they have competitions, or tests. The choirs sing to prove which is best! One time I saw a woman who was a lead soloist but who was losing her voice. And here came a young soloist in another choir. We watched a contest, the old soloist trying to maintain status. It was like watching seals on a beach, you know, to see who's the boss, the beachmaster, that kind of thing. And the audience watches. They have their heroine. I have watched an old gentleman named White, who is an elder at the Arredondo Church. He works on campus. I've seen his face. And one time he stood up, the old white-haired fellow, and he sang. You should have heard—because he was singing "old fashion," and the old fashioned way is disappearing. The young people aren't learning "old fashion," but they knew what they were hearing. He would sing (we could almost hear him thinking his next line). He would chant. The youngsters chanted in response. And he would chant longer, louder. And then when it finally was done, oh, how they did applaud! That audience knew that they were hearing the real goods! It should have been recorded.

Kramer: I once worked in New Orleans (over 30 years ago), and when I went back to "N'awlens, Loosianuh," two years ago, I was anxious to hear New Orleans jazz which I had heard then, and liked. I have since heard other forms of jazz, but they almost all lacked something—so did modern music, rock and roll, and the like. Two years ago I stumbled on Preservation Hall, where, I later learned, old-time black jazz bands come to play from about 8:30 until 1:00 in the morning. I went the next night. It's an old shack of a building, with only wood benches, lots of people standing or sitting on the floor. And the bands play away—number after number. The musicians are 50, 60, even 70 years old. When I heard that music, God, I had tears in my eyes because I knew it was "the real McCoy," and I was glad it was still around. I knew that there had been something around of which almost all modern jazz had become a distortion. How many times had I listened to it—not many, and yet I knew the real thing as soon as I heard it. I often tried to describe the difference, but didn't succeed. Now I know what it is—modern jazz, for the most part, is too intellectual. Really basic jazz comes from people's guts. I've made the same criticism about some art—it's too intellectual.

Williams: That is true. But the "gut realization" is a formal realization. One of the qualities you will find notable about the Arredondo congregation is their sense of formality. Just as Henri Rousseau, the naive painter, has some of the most formal 20th century work, and Grandma Moses, who didn't know the word, is utterly formal in the positioning of buildings, cattle, etc. After all, art is forming. And what these people do in the way of intuitive forming, we as intellectuals have to do as I have to do, you know, form conceptually.

Kramer: But you don't work only conceptually, because as you mentioned, when you start a work you may have a conception but it changes. Other processes are operating.

Williams: But I also have a potential that no primitive can have: one only a sophisticate can have. What I'm trying to say, I think, is how basic formality is and how I respect it in its more naive manifestations. Grandma Moses simply could not conceive nor could she begin to do what people such as you and I can do. And that is a fact. Thus, when we admire the person from the Arredondo Church who sings in such a wonderfully primitive way, there is no comparison to the sophisticated and marvelous tenors who sing at the Metropolitan Opera. Now, we are talking about a different order.

Kramer: You have brought out in the open a couple of things I think are important. One is the place of form in art, and two, what art and religion have in common, namely the experience—the personal experience of the participant. You are reaffirming in art, just as I think we will eventually reaffirm in religion, that a *religious belief system is not adequate.* That is why religion as a spiritual aspect of man is falling aside; it has become, in a sense, in this case in the worst sense, so formalized that it no longer contains the potential or the possibility for personal religious experience.

Williams: I saw a headline somewhere this week that read, "Don't tell us about religion, tell us about God." Of course, the experience with God will have its form. We won't have to search for it. It will simply be there.

Kramer: In your work, you want the experience of the participant to be as vital as the experience of the artist.

Williams: At its best, the formality of my work would develop honestly out of the idea—the formality would appear in support of the idea.

And this would lead, I think, to what I would wish—a direct encounter and experience between my art and the beholder.

Kramer: What painting in this room, Hiram, would you say meets that criterion most successfully, or that you are particularly pleased with? Tell me something of the idea that you want to convey, and how the two fit together—how the formality and the concept go together.

Williams: The "Chorus Line" is a paintint of *event*. In the painting of "The Three Women" you are particularly confronted by the woman on the right.

Kramer: I hadn't seen "Couples" before I came in this room, and I think it is very successful; I wonder why that is so?

Williams: I think it is very formal. I have tried—you know the old story of trying to get more with less—to suggest with economy that two people are there, an experience of confronting. I feel that in this painting it is strongly so.

Kramer: You said something last time about attempting to portray people who are related to each other as people. And I think that particular painting achieves that. You have a sense that they are related. It doesn't matter if that relationship is a good one or a perfect one, or whatever. But you do get a sense of relatedness.

Williams: They are in the same boat.

Kramer: I know that relatedness is the idea that you wanted to get across, from talking to you last time. At the same time, in terms of the formal nature of the painting, I feel that the painting is very successful with the silver background and just the flesh tones of the people, faceless as they are except for the nose of the male and the breasts of the woman. It conveys their relatedness and somehow the whole thing fits very nicely. When did you do that?

Williams: Perhaps 12 weeks ago. I did a series. What you see is that this reads as a configuration of two figures, a male and a female. And as we are reading it as male and female, we are also reading it as shape. And while we see flesh we are reading surface, so you are always reading it in a dual way.

In "The Irradiated Man" I wanted to image man's capacity for survival. I've accepted my work as literary. No use beating around the bush about this. I want you to know that this is a human being. I want you to know him. It would be inconceivable to show this fellow burning—that would be illustrational. But to show a man after he is burned can be a formally related sort of thing.

Kramer: So the theme of human survival under the worst ecological conditions is your aim here?

Williams: Now over here in "Doomed Man" are two mouths. I'm trying to portray a figure that has emerged from a terrible disaster—an automobile wreck, a bomb has fallen, something awful has happened—and hence the stunned look. I am very well aware that I am creating a blankness, a stunned look. It grew out of the idea. It is a shock-look. People who are still conscious when violence is visited upon them always show surprise. The look says, "It can't happen, but it has happened to me." In this sense, this image is quite literary. In a formal sense, we see two points working one above the other, against the mass at the bottom, a triangulation working against two planes.

Kramer: That also fits into the theme you spoke about earlier, the fact that no matter what kind of human being or expression we meet up with, we are never surprised. We accept it as being human, and in a sense, what you are conveying here is that even though this man is shocked and surprised, this is also part of the human condition. Even though we only rarely experience it, it is part of the background of our lives.

Williams: If I am successful, Sol, I would want you to see the painting and say that it is true, even if you had never seen this in real life. You would know this is true.

Kramer: I could make that evaluation even though I have never had that experience myself. That is where you are tapping the unconscious knowledge of every individual.

Williams: The horror of violent fate, I suppose, is built into our genes.

Kramer: The capacity for the expression of horror—perhaps we have experienced horror in our lives. You think of the horror of a child of age four who has dropped his ice cream cone. He reacts with horror, or with displeasure. But the intensity of the reaction is there. It may be what we adults consider a trivial event. The capacity for the reaction and the actual reaction often take place at that level. So what we may be drawing upon are experiences that are buried in our unconscious. Even though they be trivial, the horror would be the same. And that is what we use to say that is valid, or that is true, or whatever.

Williams: We do this all the time. As in that little essay of mine you looked over, that says that Bacon's subject is *trauma*. A truth. When I put the image there, you read it. Nor do I think that you will dispute it. You know that Hiram is right. It must be that we have this experience day in and day out. In our reading? Really, how much of our experience is vicarious. We read and know that what we read is true.

Kramer: Perhaps the vicarious experience is an affirmation of something that we have experienced.

Williams: I'm trying to support what you've been saying, that it must be that we know this is true because in living we have somehow touched on this; otherwise we wouldn't know what is being said.

Kramer: I remember one of Jung's students (an analyst who wrote *The Wellsprings of Creativity*) mentioned the fact that in order to be a total, integrated person, one had to accept what he called the "black" part of ourselves. If you only tried for the idealized part of yourself— tried to push the black part of yourself out, you would be cutting half of yourself out of your own life. In that sense, you would not ever become a total being because you would only be utilizing or affirming part of yourself.

Williams: This is what was wrong with my dad, the Baptist minister. The struggles my father had with Satan all his life, trying to refuse the "black self."

Kramer: Right, and this chap said, you've got to know and accept the black; that's part of you too. Without the "black" part of yourself, the other part can't operate effectively or even humanely. You will only distort the other part if you don't accept the black part. So it is the black part *and* the idealized part of ourselves which enable us to function. The reason I am saying that is because I feel that what you are doing, in a way, is calling attention to areas that people don't commonly experience, but which are necessary to know to be a human being.

Williams: That is quite right. I don't feel I am a morbid person, but I think somehow there is a truth here that has to be explored.

I once said something like this, and I have repeated it a number of times when the occasion popped up. I said that I understand schizophrenia because I am schizophrenic; I understand paranoia because I am paranoic. Still, I think of myself as being reasonably "balanced." I don't subscribe to the notion that I have had the fullest experience of schizophrenia, but I have had emotions when I have been so far away from myself and reality that I once drove a car aimlessly around and around a suburban block until someone stopped me for acting peculiar. I was unaware of it—this happened during a very difficult time in my life. I don't think this was outside the "normal range," for I had been driven to this extremity. And as for paranoia, a while ago we were talking about our superior selves, and heavens, this is an admission that at the slightest praise we get "swelled heads."

Kramer: I think that we've all had that experience. Now that you mention it, I remember a time of great emotional turmoil when I was sitting listening to, I guess it was a quartet playing chamber music. Suddenly I began to hear the music in my leg. Not with my ears, but with my leg. Well, I felt, God, I understood what a schizophrenic must experience—you know, individual voices coming out of different areas, etc.—the distortion of perceptual mechanisms and the mixing of proprioceptive and perceptual mechanisms that occur in such individuals. Maybe most of us experience something like this momentarily at times of stress. With continued stress you can begin to understand the people who react more often in this way. When the proportions go beyond a certain point, we label them as being disturbed, or mentally ill.

Williams: Do you suppose the creative person, whatever the area, might have to have these identifications with human experience, but somehow maintain the integrity of self in order to trap them into form? As you know better than I, a schizophrenic's art is notable for its lack of unity. And one of the signs by which we know fine art is that it is unified.

Kramer: Something about what you just said has validity. Hiram, when I was acting as an LSD psychotherapist and had LSD sessions myself, I remember at one point in the therapy I had the impulse to do something very irrational. I couldn't bring myself to do it, because I couldn't break out of my own rationality. It was a very simple thing; I had the impulse to put my arms through my body, to the back of my body. I wanted my arms to go through my chest and back there. This impulse came up, and of course I couldn't do it because I felt it was so irrational. To have done it, I would have had to cross the bridge into the realm of irrationality. Well, I succeeded. I did cross that bridge, and I allowed myself to go through what I thought were the motions. Someplace within my body this came up, to go through the motions of putting my arms through my body to the back. I allowed myself to do the completely irrational, and within a minute after I allowed this to occur, my whole body felt marvelously light and integrated, and just right and perfectly normal. In other words, I permitted the moment of irrationality. After I had that experience, I found that I was no longer afraid of irrationality, because I felt that I could be irrational for a moment and I wasn't enslaved or captured by it. Neither did I fear it. And in terms of understanding patients, I now understood more abut the motivations of some of their behavior. But I think the major thing was that I was freed of the fear of irrationality. And I don't know if that fits in with something you are saying, but the fact is that you could have these irrational moments of sensitivities and accept them, and even work from them and not fear that you are losing your rationality, or the other aspect of it. In other words, it allows you to easily accept your own moments of irrationality. Why not explore them, which I'm sure every artist must do in some ways? Doesn't he sometimes get into these areas? And then draw upon them for material?

Williams: I think because of the nature of the kind of image I work at, I am not as free as, for example, Pollock. He had a wide visual possibility, and a wide range of color. He could utilize his entire body as an artist. His art permitted him extraordinary latitude. Of course, I am not allowed such freedom by reason of what I do.

Kramer: As you pose the artistic problem, it is different from the way Pollock poses the artistic problem.

Williams: That's correct. Remember when I talked about identification? My experience with the "skins" led me so far toward violence that I had to stop the damned things because I was afraid—there was a point where I had to do violence with them and without them.

Kramer: I was going to ask you about that. Now in view of the experience that I have just enumerated, where I permitted myself to do the completely irrational, it was a struggle, mainly because I'm quite a rationalist. (You know, maybe that's why I am a scientist, because the rational form, in scientific terms, excites me!) It was a struggle, but I allowed myself to do it. And not only that, it opened the door to an interesting aspect of myself that I was not aware of—it was the fear of going into the irrational. In your art work when you say you were getting so close to the "skins" that you found you couldn't control what you were going to do, I wonder if the thing to do isn't to explore that even more? Aren't you being blocked by some deep, vital fear?

Williams: I won't suggest that this is true of all artists, or even any of them other than myself. I have certain inhibitions, no question about that. Maybe it is because I am my daddy's son.

Kramer: Have you ever thought of going a little further into these areas as you come close to them?

Williams: No, because my feeling is that I haven't gone far enough in this semi-rational imagery. If I came to the conclusion that I had terminated this imagery I don't know where I would go then. I have a sense of withdrawal. For example, I dislike both German abstraction and expressionism. And I don't like painting in which marks seem to be a good deal random. I am reasonably neat. As I get older, as I leave the house, I insist on my bed being made, and I would be annoyed if the rug were dirty. This is something—aging, or perhaps because of war experiences—consciousness of cleanliness and that sort of thing. Yet, I don't think of myself as having an ordered mind. Maybe this is one of the reasons I'm with figurative work. Maybe to me this is a definition in form that my personality will allow me to accept. Making all sorts of "goofy marks" I can't do! For instance, the work of Hundertwasser, the German; do you know of him? His stuff has to do with insane art. He himself has surely taken these trips you are talking about. It is plain displeasing to me. I just can't imagine myself doing his stuff. To some degree, the results I get may be the result of some abhorrence of certain experiences. It is conceivable that you could study a lot of art as a form taking its own direction, because the artist didn't want to take the consequences of moving in that direction.

Kramer: Many therapists sometimes say to their patients, "I understand what you were able to achieve and do in your life. Now, tell me what you weren't able to achieve." This is like the "black" and the "idealized" personality; these are two halves of the same coin. What you find yourself unable to do and what you are doing are complementary. They are related to each other in a very definite way.

Interview

Stephens' Apartment
12 June 1972

Kramer: The first thing I want to say about these paintings on Bill's walls is that I respond very positively to them. This is a phase of your painting, Hiram, I like very much; this man of many facets that you have depicted, your emphasis on the fragmented individual—a single eye, the isolated nose, a moving nose—stuff of that kind. You catch man in a way that confronts and holds me. So, I want to say, this is a group of paintings I am very positively attracted to.

I am also interested in what Bill told me—that these are duplicates of some you had done earlier. Does that mean you wanted to re-do a stage of your creative work that had actually occurred earlier? How did you feel when you were doing these? Had you left this period?

Williams: There was a problem here. There was a total number of 25 at one time, done on a University of Texas Research Grant. I destroyed a number of those paintings for various reasons: one that I call "Angry Man" I had decided looked much like a Francis Bacon, both in spirit and in open-mouth; I destroyed "Intellectuals at Impasse" because I felt it was too illustrational. The fact is I was awfully tired at the time, at the end of four months of really strenuous effort. Later I came to regret it. Bill Stephens had been on the scene throughout this enterprise. He joined me in Gainesville roughly ten years later. Bill understood that I had certain regrets and each canvas of Utrecht linen you see here was stretched by Bill. He brought them to me and I drew in the image I had destroyed ten or eleven years earlier; then he filled in the areas—a sort of Ruben's factory business. He brought the filled-in canvas to me and I began painting. Well, I found out that it wasn't so simple, but the solid surface Bill had given me reduced the painting time considerably.

Now, the fact of the matter is that if you compare what you see in the way of illustration in the *Texas Quarterly*,* you will find that in none is an exact duplication of what I had done before, because, as you have already guessed, I couldn't do it. I wasn't the same man. I wasn't in the same place. I wasn't dealing with the same image.

Kramer: The emotional background and involvement were no longer present.

Williams: That's right, and I had to develop another approach and involvement. Each of these paintings I conceive to be a bonafide Williams, but they are not at all the paintings of 1958.

Kramer: Now let me ask you something specific. This one is the equivalent of "Intellectual Man"? In what way does this differ from the first painting of "Intellectuals at Impasse"?

Williams: In the new painting there is no head distinguishable as an individual man in a crowd. And I discovered when I tried to duplicate the first painting what had put me out of sympathy with the picture was the fact that each head illustrated an individual.

Kramer: Do you recall specific difficulties encountered when doing the second group?

Williams: The difference in scale. "Intellectuals at Impasse" is about the size of the original. "The Man Under An Umbrella" is considerably less in size. "Angry Man" is much smaller; the original was six by eight feet. I was disturbed by the change in scale. If I had

---

*Volume III, Number 1, Spring, 1960.

used scale identical to the first group, it is conceivable that I could have repeated the same images.

Kramer: What you are saying is that your feeling as you are doing it, the decisions that you make with regard to something—like the size of the painting, and what you are going to do with the painting—form a unity and integrity of their own. When you disturb one element, for example the size, that unity and integrity is shifted, causing a shift in emphasis everywhere.

Williams: It's a difficult adjustment.

Kramer: Yes, it is! What I want to ask is when you did shift the size and tone down to the scale of that painting, "Angry Man," for example, you were faced with a *new* problem—you had to unify and integrate feelings within a different scale?

Williams: It had to achieve its own integrity.

Kramer: Now, how did you resolve it? That's what I want to know.

Williams: In each case it was only resolved at the point where the painting itself, in process, took on its own identity, provoking its own problems. You will notice, for example, that "The Man Under The Umbrella" presents a back view, a side view, and a front view. It became a different painting because I introduced the multiple nose, a feature not present in the first painting. "Angry Man" and this one—each of these were painted two or three times after Bill had filled them in, in my intent to locate the presentational mode for its being. God! The original idea and the original motivation had simply been lost. I could give you the idea, but I couldn't give you the motivation, or the sensibility, or the matrix out of which the painting was fabricated.

Kramer: You are saying, then, that when you go back and attempt to duplicate works you have done earlier, you really don't do that. You start and work out a new problem—the element that is new, of course, is *you*.

You may have had the old idea, but the fact that you had changed quickly made this painting another problem, another creative act.

Williams: We cannot come this way again.

Kramer: That is quite interesting of itself because I've always had a feeling that an artist starts off with a conception, and before long his painting begins to talk back to him. Whatever the original conception, as the painting talks back the conception changes, and soon you are doing more things than just your idea—a combination of your initial idea, plus what your body put on the canvas, what you are feeling, and the sense of who you are at the given moment—all that starts to talk back and affect you.

Williams: You've heard me say it. It's a dialogue.

Kramer: What you ultimately achieve when you say a painting is completed is that you work out a problem, or something you feel, and the thing that is satisfying is the achieved integration—the unity of the painting which speaks to you.

When the painting speaks to you of being complete, what does that do for you? Does that help integrate *you* as a person?

Williams: It might. The sense of having achieved the finality of this form—one is unburdened. I don't know if I have a further unity in myself, or growth of myself, but perhaps I've liberated myself for the next move.

Kramer: When you speak of growth and liberation, it seems to me a person rarely gets to express himself as a unified, totally integrated individual—that is something that is open to the artist. When you complete a painting you have fully expressed yourself for the moment, for the time. Something has come out in totality.

Williams: Le Corbusier says that the artist has the satisfaction of feeling, occasionally, that he is *larger than other men.*

Kramer: When you say larger, do you mean more fully integrated?

Williams: More God-like.

Kramer: When you are unified within yourself—if we believe in both natural biological laws and cosmic laws—you are integrated and unified with the universe, aren't you? You are unified in a way that is difficult to achieve with local conditions: one's task, one's family, they are often a matter of compliance.

Williams: I compromise in my dealing with the academic world, my job, my family. However, I carry with me this gladsome feeling that I do not compromise in my art. This is a very happy situation for me. I make a folder, for example, for Mary Ann Pofahl's dance school my way—hands off on her part. I utterly reject anything that introduces compromise when my art is concerned.

One time in Texas I mounted a sell-out landscape show. They were bought avidly. It was a happy experience. The following week I wasn't through with the idea and I returned to painting landscapes, but it was as if I were painting dollar signs. I couldn't do it. This doesn't suggest that I am more honest than others. Having an inviolate situation is something that I apparently need for mental health.

Kramer: In other words, when you did those landscapes to begin with there was no conception of success, but once you were successful as a landscape artist you began to think of yourself as a success and it interfered with the very thing you were doing.

Getting back to the paintings on these walls. I react very positively to the back and frontal view of this image ("Turning Figure," 1958). How many years is this after the period when you first started this theme?

Williams: The first image was realized in 1958. This, as a matter of fact, was the least of that group. I was close to throwing it away and Bill Stephens liked it and wanted it, so I handed it over to him. I suspect that may be the start of his collection.

Kramer: It is interesting that among all these paintings, "Turning Figure" is the one I am most attracted to. Did I pick up something about it that had the *original intent*?

Williams: Guess so. This painting ("Playmate") is the roughest "Chorus Line" I've done. I have been more successful, but this one of Bill's is the prototype of what was to follow, and for that reason may deserve existence.

Kramer: In these "chorus lines" and such, when did you first start hanging legs outside the frame of the canvas?

Williams: In 1967.

Kramer: At the time you had started the idea of the chorus line and the paintings that got out of the frame, you were repeating?

Williams: I had great difficulty violating the sanctity of that tyrant, the square.

Kramer: As I consider these two periods of your development, I wonder, what if you had done the moving man ("Turning Figure," 1958) in the mode of the chorus line ("Playmate," 1967)? It seems to me that the legs of these men would lend themselves to the legs of the women in your chorus line. What if you had combined these two ideas at that time?

Williams: It would have been too extravagant for me. In 1951 I had painted a picture which is the prototype of everything I've done in the way of these images. It is now hanging on the ceiling of a book store in Los Angeles. This was before "Pop Art." I used the silhouette of a head in a bowler hat, going above the frame. I showed it in a faculty show at the University of Southern California and got absolutely no response. It wasn't until a phone call, made two years ago, to Edward S. Peck, that I learned that the painting had indeed caused excitement, but no one had bothered to tell me.

Kramer: Are you saying that years after you had done the painting it caused excitement?

Williams: No. It caused excitement at that time. It disturbed people. They didn't know how to react. "Pop Art," the educational, the conditioning process, hadn't occurred. If a critic had come along at that time and recognized what I had done, I might today be recognized as a precursor of "Pop Art," but, of coure, this didn't happen.

  If only one champion—somebody to reinforce me—if one person had said, "Hiram, you are really doing something," I'd have gone ahead. But nobody showed. Therefore, I fumbled from 1951 to 1956—five years when I could have been pushing these images.

Kramer: That rings a bell with me. I have often responded in the same way as a scientist that you respond as an artist. When I first came here, there were many areas of biology and behavior and human biology, medicine within me. But it took somebody to say, "Won't you come here and do this for me," or "Won't you write a paper." All the papers I've written in biology and medicine have been by invitation. I view this as a detriment to my own growth and development. I wait for other people to ask me to do things. I'm presently trying to embark on doing things for myself.

Williams: When we look at the art scene, which is primarily in New York—and in a secondary way, London—we find heroes for the last fifteen years have been the Rauschenbergs, the Jasper Johns, etc. There is nobody in this country right now that is more productive than Rauschenberg. And Johns moves, and so it goes. The point is, they have signal success—everytime they make a gesture, it is remarked upon. No wonder Picasso was so productive—much of it not of high order, I must say. Such artists know everything they do will achieve instant response. The notion that the artist in the attic, if left alone, turns out great art is nonsense. History shows us that the artist who turns out significant things has had significant support.

And my significant support down here are people like you, and my students, who, of course, expect a lot of old Hiram. They keep an eye on me. But what I might be doing if I had real critical attention! I think I might do significantly more, although I can't prove that. Public success day after day, I think has yield, and is invaluable to creative artists.

Kramer: Even the artist doesn't work apart from the social environment.

Williams: I ran into a fellow, Bill Stephens, who has watched as I have come into doing these images, who has waited sometimes with baited breath to see what would come of what I was doing. I know his admiration is absolutely selfless. I think in some surrogate way I am his creative self—I won't propose to understand this, but he has arranged material for me to work on when he has been practically poverty stricken. The biggest implication of this situation is his sheer desire for it. And I couldn't deny him. He is my waiting and much interested public.

Kramer: So when you are asked—

Williams: The tendency is to give.

Kramer: I think what you are talking about is trampling on all levels of life. Very often the best of what we have to give is what we consider to be the most vital part of ourselves. Then if there is nobody to take that, nobody to ask for what we want, we feel that as an individual we are not really appreciated or related to other people. So, I can well understand that if somebody asks you specifically—

Williams: Sol, it can work the other way. One can work creatively when one has been rejected by a group or a critic. If he convinces himself that those who have rejected him are contemptible, it can become a motivation. One gets his back up.

Kramer: There are two prods to creative work. I think of somebody like Freud, for example, in medicine. He was rejected by physicians. They thought his stuff was junk.

Williams: But didn't he have someone who accepted him and understood?

Kramer: I don't think he did. As far as I know, there was no one who really lauded or accepted his material, apart from the patients he worked with and with whom he achieved a measure of success through his methods. He would cure them of their hysterical neuroses and manifestations of disturbances. So there was positive feedback from that. He knew he was doing something important, certainly, for the people that he treated. And there were individuals with whom he carried on an intellectual dialogue and exchange, like Wilhelm Fliess, who was another physician, not in the same class as Freud, but at the same time these two exchanged ideas and concepts. Apparently Fliess appreciated a lot of what Freud had to contribute, and that was often a center around which their dialogue revolved. Freud did have that, but he didn't have acceptance in the eyes of his professional colleagues. He was often laughed at when he presented papers.

Williams: The reason I brought this up is that I've worked when in an "I'll show them" attitude; knowing there were one or two out there who were responsive to me meant the difference. To be totally rejected could be a horse of another color, could cause impotency in the creative person.

Kramer: When I started my own scientific work, for example, I always had one or two people who liked what I was doing and thought well of my work. That helped. When lay people said, "What are you going to do with insect morphology and evolution? There is no money in that." That didn't bother me one bit because the people who appreciated my studies were all world authorities. All I needed was the support of one or two such people to persist.

Williams: But they had to have authority?

Kramer: I respected these individuals. I thought a lot of their capacity and ability. I knew that what I was doing answered *their* criteria of creative work; that got me through everything. I did need one or two people to measure myself by. That's where the environment does make a difference in what is brought out in you.

To get back to these paintings which were done over ten years ago—when did you start this group of paintings? In the early fifties?

Williams: The very first imagery occurred in 1951. Then there was an interval until 1956. In a creative life five years is a long time. In 1956 I again became interested in the image; I can't tell you precisely why. In the fifties, if one weren't an abstract expressionist one was nowhere. It was an ethical situation presumably, and the pressure to be nonfigurative was enormous.

Kramer: I remember that as a period when I was bothered by the disappearance of the figure. The figure of the human being and man's reaction to another human being was always central in my appreciation of painting. Of course, I appreciated the modern development, but I hated to see the figure go because I believe man's most creative aspect comes out in relation to his fellow man. I felt, for the abstract expressionist, the artist was being driven by his materialistic technological environment. He was being driven away from something very tender—feeling about another person. It doesn't matter if that feeling is violent or angry, etc. The mere fact that you show yourself capable of getting excited about another human being is what counts. So I viewed, with a certain amount of regret, the artist being driven away from his concern with his man to man, or man to woman relationship. Anyway, what you are saying is that you never really lost this relationship.

Williams: We talk constantly of the artist being individual, creative, etc., but no less than other men, he is a herd animal.

By and large, the people in art, I regret to say, are noncreative; and the tendency is to run with the avant garde herd. There will be a few pioneers, but when the smoke is cleared away you will find that there has been a whole generation of painters who have been doing nothing but rehashing someone's style.

In 1950 deKooning began his "Women" series. I cannot honestly tell you that I was aware of them at the time. I know that well back there deKooning's "Women" were supportive of what I was doing. When Dubuffet came along with the "Corp de Dames" series (1958-1959), that was supportive. Andrew Wyeth was supportive—I found any capable figurative artist to be supportive.

Kramer: What impressed me about deKooning's "Women" was that he was endeavoring to go somewhat along the abstract pathway. But he didn't lose the image. He certainly abstracted his "Women," and he abstracted the relationships and emotions one felt about them, but they were still there.

Williams: I remember an excerpt from a talk deKooning gave at the Museum of Modern Art. He said, "It is not true that you can no longer paint a man leaning against a lamp post." My reaction to this was: Of course! This is no news! But to hear an artist of deKooning's calibre make a statement directly into the face of Clement Greenberg and company was encouraging.

Kramer: I remember my very positive reaction to the first Dubuffet show I saw some ten years ago. I was so impressed with Dubuffet at the time. In light of what you have just said, I realize now *why* I was impressed with Dubuffet. Because Dubuffet saw man and woman in all their sordidness, in all their grotesqueness, in all their distortions. In spite of these distortions, they retain tremendous sensitivity. He didn't give up his relatedness to them—in other words, he stayed with them. You know, in older times when a person drew someone it was with regard to his concept of beauty. What I admire about Dubuffet is that he saw human beings as so imperfect, so distorted by their environment, but he stayed with them. And in staying with them, in the confines of the canvas, he manages to create something beautiful.

Hiram, in some ways you have done the same thing. You see man in his distortions. You see women used as sex symbols, but you don't abandon them.

Williams: To abandon my imagery would be tantamount to leaving myself. My image of man is my image of myself. I believe, however, that the beauty you see in Dubuffet lies in his formality and use of material, hence his brutal comments become appetizing.

That's why the Ash Can School managed beautiful paintings of ash cans, cats in dirty snow, etc. In any format where there is an achieved unity there is beauty.

Kramer: I think of the themes that I'm getting into now in mysticism, and also old time mythologies, and what they endeavor to reconcile—the opposites that were present in man and the universe. In one sense Dubuffet does this. He takes human distortion and grotesqueness, and in spite of them he produces a beautiful canvas. My feeling is that you have done the same thing. In spite of man's multifacetedness, his distortion, you still produce what I consider to be beautiful creations from an artistic point of view.

In a way that is at the heart of all mystical transcendence. You transcend one aspect of man, and you are able to come to realize the other aspect.

Williams: Paradox is at the heart of affairs. I started out some years ago to paint the human image in the all-around. But look what happened. I now use one eye to suggest a thousand eyes, one breast to suggest a thousand breasts—the very opposite of a total configuration. And this happens as night follows day. I was required to cudgel my brain in order to come to this as I was working.

To amplify, in my intent to do the one, I do the opposite. (If I introduce a softness in my painting, you can be sure that somehow my hand will introduce a compensating hardness.) Even though I paint the total figure, I am eventually moved to use the meagerest of means to describe that totality.

Kramer: That fits in with what I know of man biologically. The kind of an individual you are influences every part of you biologically. You can delineate character structure in your paintings because, if a person is influenced by one's totality, you, Hiram, should be able to draw one portion and depict the whole being. All people are integrated neuromuscular systems. The reason a person walks and stands the way he does is because he is an integrated muscular system. For instance, if a man has a tendency to shrink, he can't just shrink around his neck and shoulders. If he shrinks there, he changes the curvature of his spine, and the tonus of his muscles right down to his toes.

If a man is an integrated being, as I believe he is, and all his experience and background is reflected in his totality, then he can't change one part of himself without changing the whole.

Once when talking with Konrad Lorenz about Darwin's neuromuscular appraisal of grief, he said "you cannot only tell a grief-stricken person by his eyes, you can tell a grief-stricken goose! A goose that has lost its mate goes around for months afterward with a grief-stricken face." How does Konrad Lorenz read a grief-stricken face? It's largely in the eyes, because that dejection in the total body ultimately affects what we call the light in the eyes, the way the eyes look, and that difference can be recognized.

When you take two eyes, as you have done in this painting, you reflect the whole individual. You are right on the ball there.

Williams: Seldom do lay people inquire as to missing facial features. I give them one or two features and they supply the missing features through imagination.

Kramer: We read bodies much more than we admit to ourselves. For instance, you and I converse. We are conversing in symbolic speech. But that's not our only mode of conversing. We also converse on a body, eye, facial level.

Your painting supplies the cue. Your audience is utilizing its own background and understanding of that cue to fill in that painting.

Williams: I do expect them to read a real human being there, in a literal sense, along with whatever art is there.

Kramer: You know, there is a movement today in theatre where the ending is never spelled out. You are left hanging. At the end of the piece there is no resolution to the problem. The audience is left to consider its own solutions. In a sense you are doing this—you are asking the viewer to participate in the creation.

Williams: I'm asking him to supply a great deal of the image. The burden is upon the viewer.

Kramer: Hiram, let's get back to your trying to recapture your 1958 images. I often run across periods of an artist's work that I especially like, but I come along after that period is over; and I would like to have a painting from the artist's earlier period. But I know I can never ask an artist to go back. I have to accept the fact that I have missed the boat!

Williams: One can't do it in a literal sense.

Kramer: Right. The person is different.

Williams: Yes, and technically most of us don't pre-plan. We process paintings. Most of my paintings I couldn't reconstruct, because they may have achieved identities three or four times during the processing. Many times I've signed a painting; then the next day I have completely redone the painting, and it would have nothing to do with the one I had signed the day before. I'm sometimes lazy—I may not have painted out the signature, I just left it there.

Kramer: I've gotten into something like that in scientific writing. I lose two pages of manuscript. Do you think I can write those pages the same way? I can't! I remember once page 59 was missing. Well, page 59 depended on the first 58 pages for the whole continuity and flow. After I had finished the paper I couldn't write page 59 the same way, and I knew it. I just tore my hair out trying to find it and I couldn't, so I had to reconstruct it. I said to myself, "Okay, don't try to do it the same way; just do it as you feel it now. That's the only way it will be any good at all. It will be somewhat different. Accept it."

Williams: People say that I verbalize when writing or talking in a "stream of consciousness." And I agree with that, but I would like to know why it is not "stream of consciousness" when they do it. What's the difference? I feel they are saying: here is the artist, nature's ignorant child who has come along with various profundities, but unwittingly; he achieves his expression because he is utilizing his "stream of consciousness."

Kramer: Everyone is nature's ignorant child, at least once.

Williams: I would assume everybody is, so why make a point of it?

Kramer: I don't know why. When I started reading *Crime and Punishment, The Brothers Karamazov,* and that whole genre of Russian writers, I thought, my gosh, these thoughts go on in my own head. This is the stuff I think, the fantasy life, the fantasy world, the evil thoughts that go through my own mind; and this guy has written a book about them, not just the beautiful thoughts, but about the good and evil that was so much in the foreground in older times. That was a tremendous affirmation for me because, in a way, I confirmed myself as a person. I found somebody writing as I knew myself to be. You are saying, "Why make a fuss about the stream of consciousness?"

Williams: I think what they really mean is that I am not bringing a critical afterthought which they perhaps think they bring.

Kramer: That is considered to be the privilege of the creative person, the artist, or whatever he happens to be. He doesn't have so much of a damper, or rather the same repressive mechanism, to blot things out. He accepts this part of himself. One of the things Carl Jung used to say about individuals is "Why all this striving for perfection, why this striving to be good? If you only retain the goodness, what you consider to be the good part of yourself, and knocked out the evil part, you'd be half a person." Why strive to be half a person? It was only when he put it that way that I got the message. If you want to be a whole person, you had better accept the good and the evil together. That's what you are saying also, Hiram. Aren't you? The artist accepts the opposites in himself, deals with it, and works with it.

Williams: I get the impression regularly that I say things that are shameless and behave in certain ways that are shameless. To see the reactions around me, I have a sense that I do not function within the realm of approval. I'm not bizarre in my actions, yet I continually say something that good manners forbid me to say. I don't have the sense of guilt, I say, and I can't seem to stop myself even when I know there is going to be a bad reaction.

In some respects, I find it difficult to live in the world. To illustrate, during a painting session which can be extended into months, I'm almost incompetent to do much more than take the roll of a class. For example, if any administrative responsibility appears during such a time, I am patently incompetent to the task. When I edited the faculty year book, I gave up painting for a year, which is a strange thing. The mind that did the one simply could not do the other. When sitting in a committee I can't think about my art, or any art, for I have a sense of fuzziness and removal, and rebellious thoughts stir me, although I try to comply and be a useful agent for society, etc.

If there is any constant in my life, it is a sense of walking removed from my fellow man. I'm sure I fit a psychological type and that the hospital is full of them, but I tend to think of it as being in the nature of what I do and what I am because of what I do. I mean, I don't think I do what I do because I am, but what I do *shapes* what I am. When I stop doing what I do, I can join the next man and be a good committee member, lead a company in the war, etc.

Kramer: You can't do both—you can't do both and be true to your own sense of what you do and who you are.

Williams: I have a sense of being set apart. I also tell you this, something I haven't voiced to anyone. I see myself as an hysteric! For example, my reaction to the fact that we have almost hit somebody while my wife was driving the car was instantly hysterical. It's strange, becasuse I don't have a sense inside myself of being in utter turmoil, but my physical and vocal aspects can only be me. And my reaction to having to deal with day-to-day matters? I've got to go get a loaf of bread we forgot—I must turn around and go back. I'm sure that any man could be miffed because he has to plod the same steps again, but my reaction too often is too shrill. What I'm saying to you is that I have a sense that this ties into my personality as an artist. What do you think?

Kramer: A lot of people play the same game with themselves about their inner nature. They cover it up. Almost everyone has a public mask. What you are saying is that you are less inclined under these trivial circumstances, as well as when you are creating something, to be different than the way you feel. If you feel a little bit hysterical, you *are* hysterical. Most of us aren't that direct. I often have a lot going on inside; I'm involved with my own problems, but like to try to work them out within myself, so I seldom bring them up for discussion. I imagine that people sometimes consider me not very communicative because I'm often tied up grappling with inner problems that I'm not solving too well on my own. I'd probably do better if I voiced things more. So that is the opposite of what you are saying.

Williams: You're very open and mature. I don't have a sense of maturity. But I despise this concept of artists being child-like. I've even heard several of my confreres in times past suggest that something was dulling their sensibilities; they weren't as child-like as they wished to be. I find that abhorrent. I'm not interested in being child-like. That's too close to childishness, I'm afraid. Conceptionally I understand what they are saying. I still do have an extraordinary sense of being a child in the world. Maybe it is because there is an element of what I do that is sheer play. It is very serious play, for I can become decidedly unhappy.

Kramer: One of the things that emerges from looking at animal behavior is that adult animals—adult primates, for example—do not play. Adult cats play with their kittens—they play-fight them, but there's a certain seriousness in that play. This is one of the things which distinguishes adults from juvenile and infant animals. As they mature they do less and less playing. Perhaps retention of a certain child-like quality is part of being an artist; but not being child-like in totality. Many artists I know have child-like characteristics, but so do non-artists.

Williams: Malraux quoted some wise man as saying, "Nobody ever grows up." Malraux felt this was a remarkable insight.

Kramer: In class, I sometimes talk about regression in psychotherapy in relation to the biological basis of character and social behavior, and my students look at me very skeptically. "How can you recover childness?" they ask. So I bring up their love-play, and remind them that the more intimate they become, the more infantile things they do. It's the childish expressions that they value most in intimate relationships.

Williams: Of course.

Kramer: I challenge the idea that regression is always something bad, or that it is only something people do in therapy. That's nonsense. Everyone lives his whole life out regressing all the time. Every time you become intimate with someone you regress; it's part of the cycle of life. To go back and come forward, to go back and to come forward. All this about being childish as some special characteristic of artists, I agree, is a lot of nonsense, because we all do it. To survive you almost have to be childish at times. That is part of being a human being.

Williams: You couldn't procreate without it. You set up the ambience for procreation.

Kramer: That's a good point, Hiram. Many animals return to juvenile behaviors during courtship. The point I'm making is that the relationship we call intimate behavior (that has nothing to do with procreation, except secondarily) is full of child-like elements.

Williams: Well, listen Sol, do you suppose for our next engagement we'll be able to find a hypnotist to put me under.

Kramer: I'm going to write Bernard Aaronson and tell him what we've been doing, and ask him about it and see what he can do. Now, the other thing is that I could try hypnotizing you. I've been hypnotized myself, and I might try that with you if we can't find someone else.

Williams: I'm sure I'm very suggestible.

Kramer: We'll try it. It's possible.

Williams: As long as you bring me out of it, it's okay.

Kramer: That's no problem. When you are under hypnosis, you are not that removed. You're in another realm; you're on another level; but you're not unaware of what is going on around you. You make contact with another level of yourself that you are not ordinarily used to, but which perhaps you, Hiram, do make contact with when you are painting. Your level of consciousness when painting may share characteristics with the hypnotic state.

Williams: Well, you work out the hypnotism, and Bill and I will work out the material. I'll do some image I have done before and while I am hypnotized you will probe me as to what I've been about.

Kramer: You could paint something completely new. It doesn't have to be specific—it could be something else entirely—that would allow us to get at the process.

Williams: Let's go to my house and I'll show you what I'm doing currently. There may be choices to be made, because Bill has given me some big stretchers and we could fix up a couple of those. I work rapidly, so within a two-hour time we could have a complete hunk of art done as you are quizzing me under hypnosis.

Kramer: Well, we'll try it. I'm certainly willing to try, because I know the process, and the state I was in. I know what was done to me, and we might try to reach that state in you.

Williams Paints Under Mild Hypnosis

Hiram Williams' Studio
22 June 1972

Kramer: I have been hypnotized several times, and what surprised me most is that you are not too different than when awake; you're not unaware of what's happening; you will not be unaware of me. If I talk and ask you something, you will respond. It isn't a state in which you are directed by me—you are directed by something inside yourself, which is closer to what you have alrady experienced but more so. The state is one which you have probably experienced before in painting. I'm sure you've been in this state and working in it before.

    Now it may possibly modify your plans to get you there and back— although you could start with that (Kramer is speaking of Williams' sketch), if it turns out that's what you want to do. It's up to you, whatever you want to do. So I'll give you certain instructions as to where I'd like you to go, what I'd like you to do. And you try to get there. Now when you get there, you'll experience certain feelings. You may decide to explore some of these feelings and build your painting around these feelings. Or you might just modify the sketch, or work on that, or abandon it. I don't know what is going to happen, but I'll ask you to operate out of that "feeling state." I think that is about it. So, if something comes up very strongly, very powerfully that you want to use, okay, go ahead. On the other hand, you may go through a gamut of feelings, or come to a certain calm or ease. You'll be the final decision-maker as to what you do.

How deep you go into it is up to you. In fact, it may not seem different than normal painting. But what I'll want you to do, if you can make contact with that level, will be different. How deep you go under, how much into it you get, will be up to you. You'll be aware of what is going on to some extent. There will probably be fadings of how important what is going on around you will be, regardless of painting. Now, what I'll do is start you off in this direction, and remember that I'll bring you out of it. So, in both instances we'll start here and toward the end when you feel your painting is finished you will automatically lie down here. And just continue to feel in that state, and I'll bring you out of it.

I don't know how effective it is going to be, whether you will respond, or not. But it will demand the utmost cooperation from you, because you may feel in the beginning that it is not any different than what you would normally be painting. But don't let that throw you. Try to just keep on with what I tell you, and stay with it, stay with it, stay with it. Throughout, try to make contact with the area I suggest to you. And then just keep on with that level. Meanwhile, there is no reason to have any apprehension or concern. Actually, it may turn out to be a quite pleasurable experience in many ways. Lie down now, Hiram, and get comfortable.

From the moment we were born we all begin reacting to needs within ourselves, as well as to people and circumstances outside ourselves. As a result, you might say, we slowly become conditioned to a way of responding. And that way of responding slowly grows into our bodies. So the way we think, our attitudes and reactions to people, corresponds to something that is always in our bodies—those beginning responses, those attitudes that after a while we forget about. That is, they become a part of our unconscious material, but they are motivating us all the time. They are driving us, providing us with goals and desires. In the state of being born we have already begun to respond. Actually at sometime in the beginning, when the fetus is in the uterus and just rocking along, bumping along, there really aren't too many cares, there really aren't too many concerns. It is rather a very pleasant kind of situation. What I'd like you to do when I ask you to close your eyes and go into this state is to imagine and try to feel, not just intellectually, but try to

feel with your whole body what it was like at the very beginning - -
how you, Hiram Williams, must have felt at the very beginning of
life before you had lots of problems, before you had lots of people
react to you, before you had responsibilities, your pressures, etc. Try
to feel what life must have been like at that time.

Now, when you go back to that state it may be that things are not
all smooth in that state. You may find that even then something
prevented you from being at ease. Try to feel those things out. Try to
feel those things out with your body. Get from your body, not your
head, what your moods are. You are to make very deep contact with
your body and how successfully you go into this state will depend
upon how intimate a contact you make with that beginning self that
is Hiram Williams at the very beginning of time. That's what you are
striving for. You may not get there immediately, or you may not fully
get there. There may be things in the way. Now, what I'd like you to
do is to spend a period, maybe five to ten minutes, trying to
experience and feel it through, some of those states and aspects of
Hiram Williams, the deep Hiram Williams, that you maintain
contact with. Keep in touch with this part and other things come up,
after a while I'd like you to begin painting from that state of your
feelings.

Whatever it is you make contact with in that realm I'd like you to
paint from that realm. Use that state of feeling. If you wish, start
with your plan and paint the painting that you planned; but only as
you keep in touch with that realm—the beginning Hiram Williams
completing this painting, or as it talks back to you.

Now the important thing is to try to get away from your
intellectual self. Try to get with this *feeling*, letting that mood take
hold. Forget about whether it is going to measure up to your usual
painting or be a continuation of some present series. In fact you may
find yourself going off in another direction. Does what I'm striving
for ring a bell with you? Okay?

What I'd like you to do now is to close your eyes and I'll begin
counting slowly from one to twenty. As you close your eyes and I
count, feel yourself as that beginning Hiram Williams was, without
present-day anxieties and pressures. If you have any unpleasantness,
try to work your way out of it, and correct it and get back to that
beginning pleasurable state. Then, when I've counted, if you don't

feel you're in a deep enough state, I may count again. Although I don't think it should be necessary because if you are not completely under at that point, just continue making contact with yourself and working; so for a period of five, ten, maybe fifteen minutes you'll be doing nothing but making contact with that state within yourself. At that point it's up to you to decide what you are going to do with your painting. So you begin, and then, although you will open your eyes, you'll see the canvases and the paints, you are not going to let that state, whatever you have arrived at, go. You'll be able to see everything around that is going on, but you are not going to let go of that particular mood; stay with that and try to find your way to that beginning Hiram Williams.

All right, we'll start now. Close your eyes and I'll count slowly to twenty. As I do that you make contact with that beginning Hiram Williams—the very beginning, before you got out into the world, and your nature and your being and your own true self, the person who really is Hiram Williams. So we'll start—one—two—three—four—five—six—seven—eight—nine—ten—eleven—twelve—thirteen—fourteen—fifteen—

Now, you are beginning to go into this state, but you can hear what I'm saying—you are aware of what I'm saying—when you reach that level there will be no difficulty in our corresponding, talking, and I may, from time to time, suggest things to you or indicate a direction you might be going, and you can either go in that direction or not, as you choose. The main thing is to maintain the state that you're in. Just keep going deeper and deeper, and gradually the feelings will change as you stay with your inner self. You'll find yourself responding, responding. You will also be aware of my voice, and anything that I say, and you will be able to react to that. You need not talk back to me, you need not express yourself verbally to me, simply continue with your painting. Express yourself in that way. Keep contact with the state that you are going into now, and I will continue counting—sixteen—seventeen—eighteen—nineteen—twenty—

Now, let's try another series of counts to twenty, during which time you will contine to make contact with this part of yourself, the beginning Hiram Williams as it was before you came out into the world with all its pressures—what life must have been like, what feelings you must have had in the very beginning. So we start again—one—two—three—four—five—

And I might add, Hiram, the beginning feelings that you have that you want to express can move through you in any way. If there is anything that wells up that you feel you want to give in to, go ahead and express it. —six —seven —eight —nine —ten —eleven —twelve—thirteen—fourteen—fifteen—sixteen—seventeen—eighteen—nineteen—twenty—

You may begin whenever you are good and ready. Just start and move in a way which will not disrupt your mood. Keep with the mood, making contact with that part of yourself, until the painting is complete.

When the painting is complete, put your paints down, your brushes down, and lie down again. Keep with the mood, or feelings, and I will bring you out of that state.

(Hiram gets up and starts to paint.)

(Thirty minutes, or so, later)

Let that early Hiram react to the canvas, to whatever you're doing—what you are *feeling*. Can you incorporate that reaction some way into your painting—and do it from a "feeling" level?

(Williams painted throughout the whole session without saying a word. He went right to work drawing the figures on the canvas as soon as Kramer signaled for him to begin, and he slowed down only when the spray cans of paint were clogged. As soon as Williams had finished the painting, he went back to the reclining chair where it had all started and Kramer went through a reverse counting procedure and brought Williams out of his hypnotic state.)

(talking together in the kitchen after the session)

Williams: Boy, am I tired!

Kramer: I thought you were. Now, when you normally do a painting, is the reaction the same? Do you have the same feeling you usually have when you complete a painting?

Williams: Yes, I work awful fast and I put a lot into it. Boy! You should have caught me when I was doing the skins—that would have been something! I knew something was going on with me then. I felt like I was a butcher. There was a time there when I was scared of me! I could see that I could carve people up, I could do anything. I've had this occur before but in a very slight sense—it was a vague sense.

Kramer: The thing you can do, you see, is let yourself go a little more into those areas, and use them and then it will come out. But, go where those things take you in the painting.

Williams: Though I've had no specifics, I've had no sense of going beyond where I've been before. For, after all, I've spent years probing this guy. You know I'm not nearly as rational about my painting as people think. I give myself boundaries, and people think, "Hiram, the intellectual." I am not. I have an enterprise that I am about, and it is so much bigger than me that I'll be damned if anything can shatter that. I'm not going to be just another child painter. On the other hand, I've been doing what I could to take myself into account, my meanness, my sense of viscera, etc.

Kramer: But what I hoped you would take into account were the very earliest of these feelings—not the present ones.

Williams: I have a terrible concern about self-expression. I've been concerned about putting you and me—mapping us—putting us there on the canvas; the real us, whatever. As in my big "Audience" painting, I'd like you to look and see it, and say, "Boy! That's us!" Not, me, *us*! There is some difference maybe between me and Van Gogh in this sense. That is a rational attitude, I understand.

Kramer: That's why I said that what you would feel is another mood— that you will feel something of experiences you have had before. I know you've been there, sometime.

Williams: Well, I express myself as if I were the rest of humanity; that's what I say I try to do, which is no novelty. Everyone of us does that. I was not nervous. (about the hypnotism)

Kramer: You didn't have any problems once you started did you?

Williams: No, not really. My only concern was, "Am I hypnotized?"

Kramer: I knew you were, but I was trying to tell you that you wouldn't think you were very different.

Williams: I know. Boy! If I'd known it was no different than this—

Kramer: The only time it would be different would be when you got to those butcher states you were talking about—to go with them more and let those direct your painting. But you already have a good sense of it, and next time you may want to go deeper.

Epilogue

No theory was set to be tested in this study; therefore there is no allegiance to any position or hypothesis. Questions which have intrigued critical minds concerned about the development of creative people were discussed prior to the start of the interviews, but no arbitrary method was established for testing them. Some of these questions were: Is there such a thing as separation of conscious and unconscious thought for the creative painter as he proceeds to paint? Is his thought, at any given time, merely a shorthand of the total thought, and is that thought predetermined by all the factors of the mind? Is his creativity only an integration and resynthesis of neuromuscular patterns of the artist's personality which result in a creative thought, a creative idea? What are the psychological and biological considerations inherent in these patterns? What are the influences that contribute to his creative processes? Is the creative painter in as close touch with his own unconscious processes when he paints normally, as when under hypnosis?

Williams was asked to discuss his painting, to expose his intimate thoughts, and speak of his rationale for communicating his versions of reality. In giving his explanations, he was able to relate his subconscious motivations and indicate what were his unconscious roots of creativity and the ways he contacted them. This approach to exploring Williams' sources of expression were amenable for consideration in terms of the results: it traced his development, what occurred with him over a period of time, and the path followed by his brain in materializing images.

Williams seemed an especially good choice for the subject of this investigation. He could translate from his behavior and conceptualize about it, and he proved extremely adroit and lucid in verbalizing his observations of self when painting.

For the skeptic, there is no conclusive evidence that Williams was in a hypnotic state during the painting session of 22 June 1972. However, evidence from other research indicates that often non-hypnotized people who are task motivated are in semi-trance state and behave much like hypnotized people.* Williams believes that he was in an altered state of consciousness, and made certain brush strokes that he normally would not have made, and Kramer considers that Williams was in a mild hypnotic state. Williams affirmed afterward that his moods and subconscious motivations when he painted "normally" were not unlike the moods he experienced under mild hypnosis.

Williams was totally absorbed in his painting at the time of the experiment. His thinking and energy were concentrated on the task before him as he moved about the studio with a sense of mission. He worked rapidly, and every stoke seemed to count. He worked with confidence, "like a metronome," he said afterward, "automatic." He had a grip on his subconscious and he worked through his sublimations and intuitions. There was apparently no separation of conscious and unconscious thought as he worked and had moments of illumination.

For some reason Williams destroyed the painting which was the spin-out product resulting from the hypnosis. He may have had second thoughts about it being sport to his repository of form and idea. However, the painting looked only marginally softer and looser than paintings he had made when not under hypnosis. To destroy the painting was not of itself an unusual thing for him to do. He said that he often painted as many as four or five pictures on top of one another. Williams worked in the belief that in the end nothing was lost because what was destroyed would turn up someplace else in his work. If he only painted to sell pictures, he would destroy nothing because, no matter

---

*Kenneth Bowers and Patricia Bowers, "Hypnosis and Creativity: A Theoretical and Empirical Rapprochement," *Hypnosis: Research Developments and Perspectives,* editors Erika Fromm and Ronald Shor, Aldine Publishing Company, Chicago 1972, p. 255.

how skimpy the marks, each picture would represent income. If Williams, like Picasso, had assistants to stretch every canvas it might have been different. In general, artists tend to over-work their canvases because they do not want to stretch another, and critics are known to write on the premise that every artist starts with an equal chance.

In April 1974 and April 1975 Williams was asked if he would consider participating in further studies of his painting while in depth contact with unconscious motivations during hypnosis. He declined, saying that things were not right for further probes. It may be that he had to halt these experiments just as he had to stop skinning objects. It frightened him to death, and he also felt that such probes would interfere with his creativity. Furthermore, the experiment appeared to intrude into his waking emotional life. He felt that he was in danger of losing contact with that unknown but dependable region of his mind that generated his art. Paradoxically, too much exposure of his "right brain" could destroy his access to it.

This study covers only a short span of time in the life of a gifted, committed American painter, Hiram Draper Williams, still painting, teaching, and working in 1978. It is hoped that this study will offer new insights into his sense of restaint and extravagance as an artist.

Commentaries

Williams' comments about his own work were recorded in notes, using longhand, by the author at the time Williams spoke them— often while Williams was in the very act of painting—others were recalled and noted a short time after conversation. The date of comment is in parenthesis (month, day, year) when it occurred in the author's notations; otherwise, the date is omitted.

Coffee Cup and Spoon (1967) (10″ x 8″)

Pointing to his coffee cup Williams said: "You realize that the cup is perfectly inanimate, yet I have a suspicion that this cup has a warmth toward me. I endow this object with my sentiments. This is just the way we relate to things in our environment." (1/15/70)

"The cup is another symbol of aloneness. Bottles and teacups can constitute images that symbolize a life of plentitude, a life of ease and comfort; but I depict them in such spare terms that, finally, I am suggesting that material plenty is in fact poverty." (1/15/70)

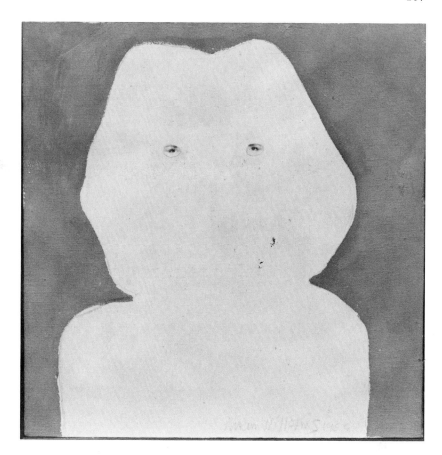

Agnes (18″ x 18″)

"You will notice that these outline heads are two or three times bigger than the size they need to be for the eyes or the nose I put in them. This, I think, gives a greater sense of space." (5/4/71)

Bill Stephens Family (18″ x 12″)

"Bill, this is the side of your head and eye on the left and this is the side of Jeanine's head and eye on the right. Below that, you are seen again after Christopher has come along, and below that are all the other Stephenses to follow. Do you suppose that Adam and Eve's last name could have been Stephens?"

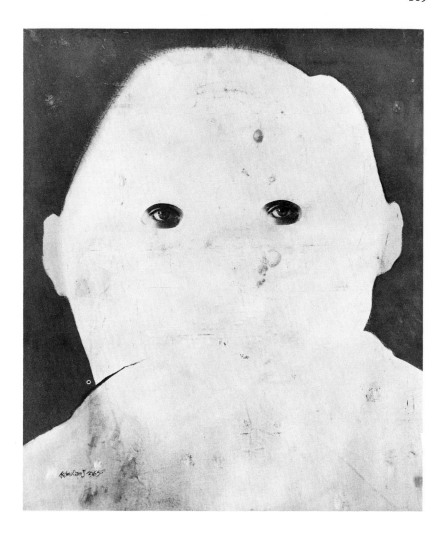

Gazer (80″ x 68″)

Made outline of male head with it in mind to have one half as figure retreating and other side as if figure were advancing. I called the image "Turning Gazer," but I've never had an indication that any viewer, ever, has noticed my ploy.

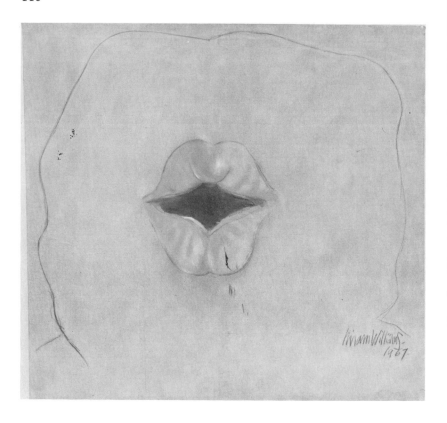

Miss Lovelorn (5′ 4″ x 5′ 8″)

This was painted in my studio in Boone, N.C. The lips are puckered, pining for love. The charcoal line describes the female head and the parted hair style. Afraid that the charcoal might get brushed off by my young son I covered it with acrylic medium, which turned the raw linen dark along the line. The whole painting was then coated with acrylic to give it an even tone.—Stephens. (12/26/67)

Talking about why he painted out one of the "mouth" series as he painted a new picture on top of it, Williams explained: "Anybody can make a painting but, like all painters I suppose, I want all mine to be salient. In this day when everything is thought to be relevant and ultimately of equal importance I am old-fashioned in that I think some works are better than others. I'm of the opinion that crap and poop are of the same thing. However, I am convinced that some craps are better than other craps, but all poops are the same." (7/18/70)

Punch Bowl (16″ x 20″)

"Through this image I am trying to say that we are all the pawns of chance. Anything can be thrown into the punch bowl and make sense. The rationality of the universe is its irrationality." (1/15/70)

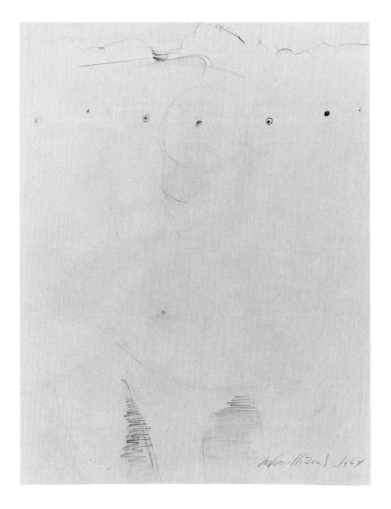

Target for Tonight (pencil sketch)

Williams and his wife came by to visit from about nine to eleven o'clock in the morning in Austin, Texas. His hands were covered with scabs, a reaction to the relatively new acrylics he was working with in Florida. I had heard about the twenty-foot chorus line from another artist and Williams made the small sketch to tell me about it:

"The nipples are targets, painted in perfect circles with hard-edge lines. This particular chorus line, twenty by nine feet, is called 'Target for Tonight.' "(5/3/64)

Crowd Gone Mad (Working Drawings for Large Painting) (24″ x 18″)

While painting in the studio: "As a painter I wish to create an exceptional work. Of course, I have trouble performing this task because, like all of us, I carry extraneous baggage, passé concepts, etc... Ideally one should simply let art happen; be free to that uniquely created line, and so forth. Trouble is one tightens up, becomes self-conscious. The sketchy line is right in this painting (crowd with flesh colored clothes, about fifteen-feet long, "Crowd Gone Mad"). The sketchy line worked properly in the crowd of heads ("Gazers," 1965). In painting, I think we should simplify, do away with confusing complications. Simplification means strict adherence to the idea; all else is extraneous." (7/18/70)

"I want to image a crowd gone mad. And I want to carry the idea of the crowd with only one face moving out from a suggestion of heads and legs. I want to lose the sense of individuals, to convey the jumbled forms of a crowd. Notice that there are images of work shoes, boots and knickers, trousers, granny shoes contained in the contour.

"The lines of movement around the main head are to articulate space, but they also shore-up the crowd-gone-mad idea." (11/25/70)

Highway (25" x 36")

    "Roads to nowhere."
    "Highways and roads *are* the American landscape."

Running Man (8′ x 6′)

"He runs. He is frightened. He is running scared—panicked." (9/28/71)

Man of the Night (6′ x 4′)

Williams made the following remarks as he worked on the painting in his studio:
"Before we are done we will have it, something right out of the Mafia. — I am
making his eyes have that Jack Palance menace. I flattened his neck to give him
more of a "bull-of-a-man" appearance. I cut in on his figure under the arm and on
the leg to give the shape more intensity." (6/3/71)

The Guilty II (8′ x 6′)

(Collection of Dalton trumbo estate)

This was painted early during the four months spent on *the Texas Research Grant*. I'd floundered about miserably during processing of two or three paintings, and it was with this one (and two or three closely allied images) that I began to come to grips with my proposal.

Any of us who apply for grants know that creating a proposal is relatively easy, usually are suggests a project of nebulous proportions and ingrediants. It is after the proposal has been accepted that the grantee comes to earth, awakens to the enormity of his obligation and feels impelled to embark upon a world cruise or join outcasts reclining along curbs in the Bowery.

I had on hand 75 yards of Utrecht linen and a barrel of paint. This was no time to become faint of heart.

Man with Bowler Hat (6′ x 4′)

Elevated view of a stroboscopic figure.

Painted two of these. The first was ruined in a gallery stockroom as a result of someone's carelessness, a huge dent was made as an object thrust against the canvas. My work accepts abrasion and other rough treatment but will not tolerate attacks from the rear.

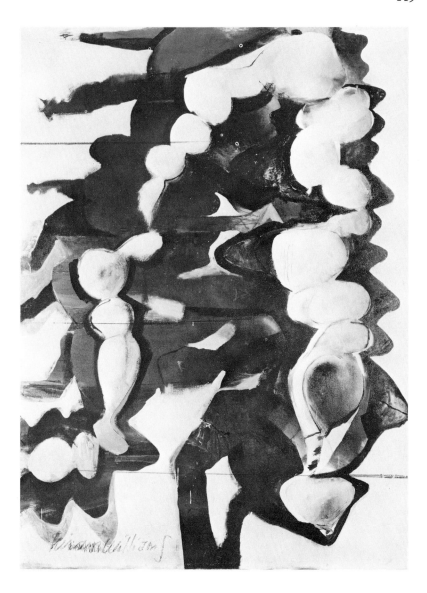

"Searcher" (96" x 72")

This was once centered in a show at the Museum of Modern Art. I forget the year. Today the University of Florida hangs it in its Constans Theatre. (1960).

Scuttling Theologian (1963)

"... Never for a moment, not for a second, do I think of them as being multi-armed, as in art representing a Hindu god. To me, even though I connect multiple arms, these to me represent continuous movements through space; and, as far as the image goes, what I offer is movement without Cubist fracturing." (7/15/71)

"... The viewer must simply accept that this is a theologian moving in space." (7/15/71)

A Crowd in Sexual Tension (working drawings) (c. 6″ high)

"Perhaps I'll find future paintings in this idea, perhaps not."

The Three Women (1959) (8' x 6')

 "... I was trying to show a woman's view of herself. I've watched my wife observing the permutations of her body." (7/15/71)

 See color plate 3.

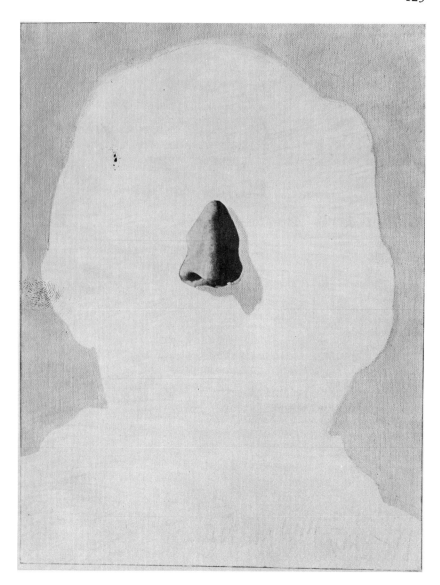

Man with Nose for Trouble (24″ x 18″)

"A nose centered in the outline of a head, which creates an illusion of human presence (or, at least, I hope so)."

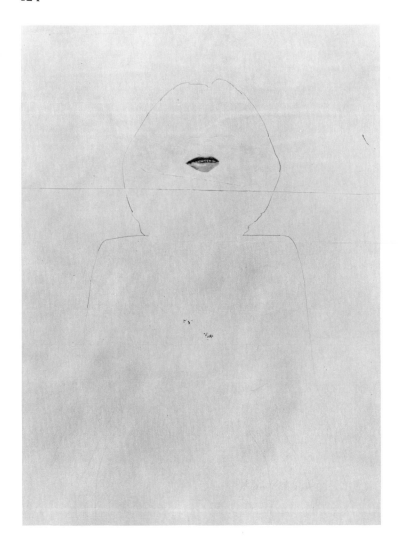

Pretty Girl with Collaged Mouth (1969) (18″ x 12″)

".. . When we look at that we don't say, where are her eyes, her nose? We *know* that is a very sexy girl!

".. . We even know she is pretty; we understand that she has a hairdo from the thirties. We know a hell of a lot about her." (8/3/71)

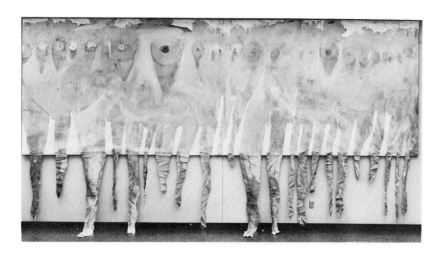

Grand Chorus Line (14′ x 21′) (Collection of the University of Texas)

"A few miles north of Gainesville, a large warehouse stores (for sale) surplus from Camp Blonding. The law permits the sale of this to groups but not to individuals. A number of us artists at the University of Florida purchased a great roll of tarpaulin—unsized, of course—and I, for one, had a field day.

"I stretched twenty-one feet along three walls of a tiny garage I used as a studio, and I painted this 'Chorus Line.' I painted a companion piece eleven feet wide. This was invited into the 1964 *Pittsburgh International,* and is now in a collection at the University of Florida."

Pink Couple

"Pink Couple is of the trio series.

"'Trio' as a title may be a little bit much. Viewers have been noticing the big breast, but haven't been noticing the reason for it. So I decided I had better make her obviously pregnant.

"Noses act as points. There is a pull between them. There is no question but that they work."

"When the couch is too fully delineated it seems to take away from the figures." (4/15/71)

While Williams was painting in the studio, I commented to him that the legs of the figures seated on the couch reminded me of his tree stump paintings of about 1955 in Texas.

"I have a feeling when I am painting new areas, that I have been there before. You noticed that the cocked-up hind leg on the bitch with stitches looked in part like the steak bones on a plate I painted back then." (6/26/71)

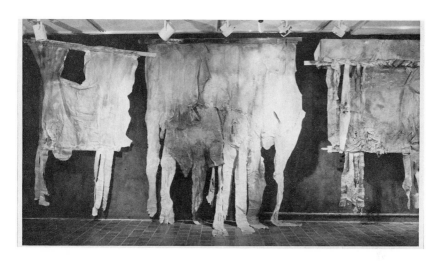

Skinned Crowd: Two Skinned Tables, A Skinned Plate, Saw and Hammer

"I cannot imagine a clearer statement about man's inhumanity toward man. A hostile New York critic scathingly wrote this was done using cowhides. He was wrong. I used seven-ounce duck from Sears, acrylic spray paint, and chiffon dipped in 'Rohm and Haas Rhoplex.'"

Intellectuals At Impasse (6′ x 8′)

"They are all, from my point of view, going nowhere. There is not much optimism, is there? These men are rendered immobile." (9/28/71)

"'Intellectuals at Impasse' are people loaded with information and the experience of the race, but—alas!—the more knowledge we obtain the less we seem capable of using it.

"What we have really learned, I suppose, if we have learned anything, is that there is no saving us from our fate. We are no longer confident—that is why the impasse. We were once confident that by amassing knowledge and by ordering experience we would come up with solutions to improve mankind's situation in the universe, to create an ideal and humane cultural ambience fit for man, that miracle among God's creations, but alas, having gained much knowledge and having ordered much of the race's experience, the academician is shocked to find the knowledge and experience as understood offers no more than testimony to man's meagerness among the galaxies and proves his activities to be futile gesturing, posturings. He is not disdained by the stars but worse—unnoticed. Man is alone except to man. The concept of "aloneness" is man's concept." (9/28/71)

"The whole idea of the humanities is to develop persons of grace and compassion—human—persons comprehending themselves, others and history. I have never understood how persons with exposure to the humanities frequently prove to be boorish and arrogant." (9/28/71)

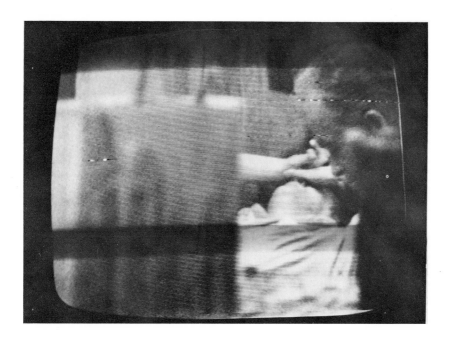

Scene from the Television Monitor

Kramer puts Williams into light hypnotic state in his studio, June 22, 1972.

". . . All right, we'll start now. So, just close your eyes and I'll count slowly to twenty. As I do that you make contact with that beginning Hiram Williams. . ."— Kramer

Scene from the Television Monitor

Williams paints under hypnosis. In less than ninety minutes he painted the eight-foot-high canvas.

Painting from Hypnosis Session (June 22, 1972)

"While I was painting I was amazed at what I was doing. I put hair on the male legs. I have never done that before, but male legs have hair on them. . ." (Wednesday Seminar, August 1972)

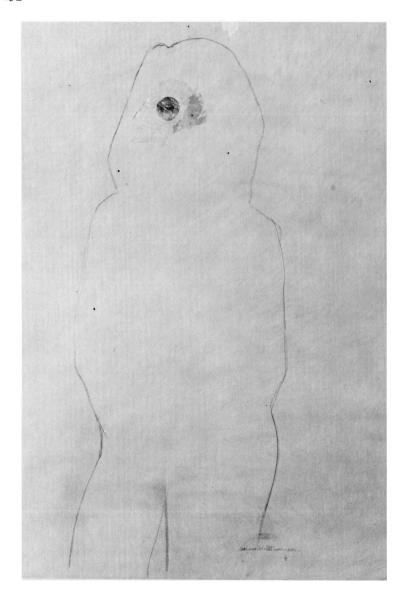

Girl with Blushing Eye (1969) (3′ x 2′)